C000258317

25.12.96

YEOVIL TO EXETER

Vic Mitchell and Keith Smith

First published July 1991
Reprinted April 1993

ISBN 0 906520 91 6

© Middleton Press 1991

Design - Deborah Goodridge
Laser typesetting - Barbara Mitchell

Published by Middleton Press
        Easebourne Lane
        Midhurst
        West Sussex
        Tel: (0730) 813169

Printed & bound by Biddles Ltd,
        Guildford and Kings Lynn

CONTENTS

ACKNOWLEDGEMENTS

We are extremely grateful for the help received from many of the photographers mentioned in the captions. Similarly, we express our gratitude to Dr.E.Course, Mrs S.Grove, A.Ll.Lambert, D.Salter, N.L.Browne P.Hay, F.Hornby, J.Petley, E.Staff, N.Stanyon, E.S.Youldon and our meticulous wives, always striving for accuracy.

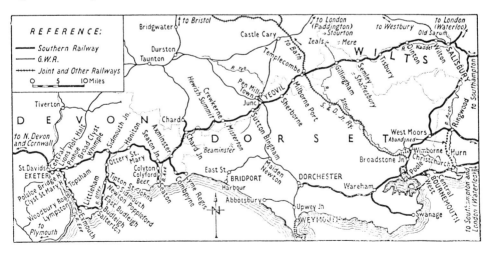

Map to show ownership of the railways
between 1923 and 1947. (Railway Magazine)

GEOGRAPHICAL SETTING

From the valley of the River Yeo near Yeovil, the line climbs past Sutton Bingham reservoir before falling into the valley of the small tributary of the Parrett, the Broad River. Near Crewkerne the route rises from an area of clays into a region of complex, much faulted, geology, chalk hills flanking the tracks. After passing through Crewkerne Tunnel the line runs down the Axe Valley for over 13 miles, before climbing over a headland to reach Seaton Junction.

A steep climb alongside the Umborne Brook follows, culminating in two miles at 1 in 80 to Honiton Tunnel. This allows the route to pass through the north-south ridge of chalk. There follows an almost uninterrupted descent to Broad Clyst, following the River Otter initially and then entering the Clyst Valley. The subsoil in this area is largely the red Keuper Marl.

In the final four miles, the line rises over a region of Lower New Red Sandstone before descending into the Exe Valley at Exeter.

The maps are to the scale of 25" to 1 mile, unless otherwise stated.

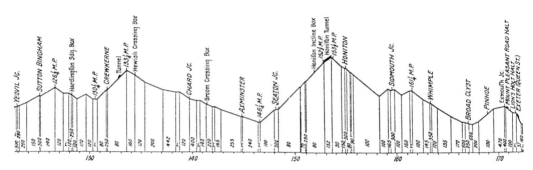

HISTORICAL BACKGROUND

The first line in the area was broad gauge and branched from the Bristol & Exeter Railway near Taunton to terminate at Hendford, on the northern outskirts of Yeovil. It opened on 1st October 1853. This became part of the Great Western Railway, as did the route from Frome to Yeovil Pen Mill, which came into use on 1st September 1856 and was extended south to Weymouth on 20th January 1857. Pen Mill and Henford were linked on 2nd February 1857.

Into this GWR territory came the rival London & South Western Railway with its line from Sherborne to Hendford, traffic commencing for passengers on 1st June 1860 and for goods on 1st September. On 19th July of that year, the route to Exeter (Queen Street) came into use and on 1st June of the following year, a new joint station at Yeovil Town was opened, in place of Hendford. The extension from Exeter Queen Street (Central from 1933) to the GWR at St. Davids opened on 1st February 1862. Laid as single track, doubling of the entire route was completed by July 1870.

Branches from the route are summarised as follows:-

From	To	Opened	Closed
Chard Junction	Chard	8-5-1863	10-9-1962 *
Axminster	Lyme Regis	24-8-1903	29-11-1965
Seaton Junction	Seaton	16-3-1868	7-3-1966
Sidmouth Junction	Sidmouth	6-7-1874	6-3-1967
Exmouth Junction	Exmouth	1-5-1861	Open

* Goods traffic continued until 3-2-1964

The route and the branches were operated by the LSWR, which became part of the Southern Railway in 1923. Upon nationalisation in 1948 the lines became part of British Railways, Southern Region, but were transferred to the Western Region in January 1963. Local trains were withdrawn on 7th March 1966 and closure of several intermediate stations took place at that time. Singling of most of the track followed in 1967.

Incongruously, the route became part of Network SouthEast in 1986 and after six years was expecting its first entirely new rolling stock for nearly fifty years. Other improvements are anticipated as the line regains some importance on the railway map.

Beattie-designed 2-4-0s were typical motive power for Waterloo-Exeter expresses in the 1860s. No.68 Apollo was built in 1846. (Railway Magazine)

PASSENGER SERVICES

The following notes refer to down trains, the up services being generally similar. Expresses not stopping at Yeovil Junction or intermediately on the route are omitted, as are newspaper trains which did carry some passengers.

Many additional trains were run for holidaymakers on summer Saturdays, notably in the years following World War II. For example, the 24 weekday arrivals at Exeter in the summer of 1954 increased to 37 on Saturdays.

The SR made an attempt to introduce a regular interval timetable but it was not until 1967 that a fairly consistent two-hour interval service started. This was associated with the commencement of electric operation of the Waterloo - Bournemouth route and the singling of much of the Exeter line. The introduction of class 50 locomotives in 1980 brought a reduction in journey times but no increase in frequency.

Sadly irregular timings were reintroduced on 21st January 1991, due to the lack of reliable locomotives, but the frequency remained as shown for 1985.

Through running of Waterloo trains west of Exeter ceased in September 1964, although the Brighton-Plymouth train continued for a while. Other western destinations had earlier included Bude, Ilfracombe, Padstow and Torrington.

	WEEKDAYS				SUNDAYS			
	A	B	C	D	A	B	C	D
1869	3	2	-	Honiton 1	2	-	-	-
1890	7	-	2	Sidmouth Jn. 2	1	-	-	-
1906	7	2	4	Honiton 4	1	-	2	Honiton 2
				Broad Clyst 2				Whimple 2
1914	5	3	3	Seaton Jn. 1	1	-	1	Honiton 1
				Honiton 1				
				Sidmouth Jn. 5				Wimple 3
1917	6	-	3	Sidmouth Jn. 5	1	-	-	-
1924	4	3	1	Axminster 1	2	-	1	Seaton Jn. 3
				Honiton 1				
				Sidmouth Jn. 3				
1934	5	4	5	Seaton Jn. 3	5	-	3	Honiton 3
				Honiton 3				Sidmouth Jn 1
				Sidmouth Jn. 4				
1944	7	1	3	Axminster 1	4	3	3	Honiton 3
				Seaton Jn. 1				
				Honiton 2				
				Sidmouth Jn. 2				
1954	9	3	3	Axminster 2	4	3	3	Seaton Jn. 1
				Honiton 3				Honiton 2
				Sidmouth Jn. 1				
				Broad Clyst 1				
1965	6	4	-	Axminster 4	4	3	-	Axminster 1
				Honiton 1				Honiton 1
				Sidmouth Jn. 1				
1975	8	-	-	Honiton 1	4	-	-	-
1985	9	-	1	Honiton 2	7	-	-	-

A - Stopping trains   C - Expresses
B - Semi-fasts   D - Starting stations and number of local trains to Exeter

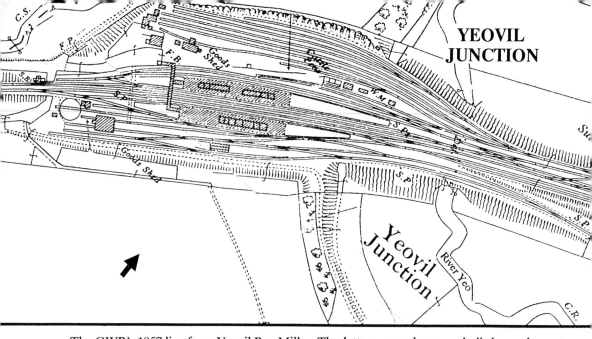

Yeovil Junction

River Yeo

The GWR's 1857 line from Yeovil Pen Mill to Weymouth runs from top right to the lower border. The trackbed of the LSWR's first route to Yeovil (Hendford) is seen on the right of the map, the service commencing on 1st June 1860. By 1869, it was used by only one train each way on weekdays. The line was lifted in the 1870s but the bridge over the GWR remained in place until the early 1930s. The LSWR main line to Exeter (right to left on this 1928 map) came into use on 19th July 1860, only seven weeks after its direct line to Yeovil.

The latter was subsequently little used, most passengers for the Town station (opened 1st June 1861) having to change at the junction. The Clifton Maybank branch was in use from June 1864 until June 1937, its purpose being the transfer of goods between the two systems. It was laid as broad gauge but was converted to standard at the same time as the Weymouth line, in 1874. The earthworks to the south of the branch have never carried track but recent proposals may reverse this situation.

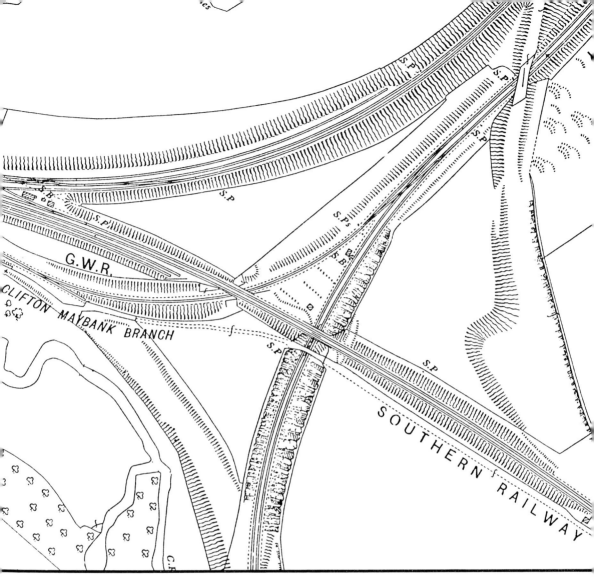

1. In 1907-09, the station was extensively rebuilt. Initially the two island platforms had a single track between them but the two new ones were separated by four tracks. Class T9 no.122 waits by the wooden signal post to depart west, during the alterations. (Lens of Sutton)

The diagram marks Yeovil Town as *JOINT PASS*. Yeovil's first station at Hendford was retained by the GWR for goods traffic, the SR having a depot at the Town station. Yeovil Pen Mill is featured in our *Yeovil to Dorchester* album, as are the later connections between the two systems. (Railway Magazine)

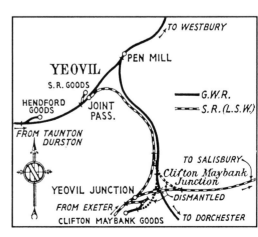

2. Lattice construction was used for the new longer footbridge and also for the new signal post. The barrow crossing was traversed by countless empty milk churns returning from London - some are lined up by the PEARS advertisement. (Lens of Sutton)

3. A westward view after the rebuilding shows the two through tracks used by expresses and of particular value on busy summer Saturdays in later years. Prior to the alterations, non-stop services had been subject to a 20mph speed limit on the curves outside the island platforms, the single line between them being used by the branch train to Yeovil Town. (Lens of Sutton)

4. Although of poor quality, this eastward view from about 1930 is of interest because it includes the GWR's goods line, curving between the telegraph poles. In its first 10 years as a broad gauge line all goods were manually transferred but later the lines were connected. Transfer of cattle wagons took place at Yeovil Town. (Lens of Sutton)

5. On 21st May 1935, the up island platform was the background for this photograph of two Maunsell designed products. The U class locomotive was extensively used on the route. The cattle pens were to the right of Bradford & Sons' coal wagon. (H.C.Casserley)

6. Eastbound with a non-stop express on 21st August 1954 is no. 34016 *Bodmin*, now preserved on the Mid-Hants Railway in the rebuilt form. The van on the left is standing on the former connection with the GWR Clifton Maybank branch, that company's goods shed being visible in the distance. (H.C.Casserley)

7. No.34098 *Templecombe* waits to head west with a long and assorted freight on 28th April 1962. These trains were generally remarshalled at Exmouth Junction. The apparent lack of signals is explained in the next photograph. Goods facilities at Yeovil Junction were withdrawn on 5th April 1965, but coal traffic remains. (E.Wilmshurst)

8. No.34052 *Lord Dowding* passes Yeovil Junction with the 2.25pm Plymouth to Waterloo relief train on Easter Monday 15th April 1963. The venerable West box survived being struck by a runaway freight train in July 1914 and remained in use until 30th April 1967. The third generation of down starting signals are seen on the left. It is clear that the track layout did not allow through running to the northern face of the up island platform at that time. It was mainly used by the Yeovil Town train. Following the singling of the route westwards at the end of April 1967, the layout was changed and the down platforms were taken out of use. It was not possible to pass trains in the station until further alterations were completed on 26th March 1975. (J.N.Faulkner)

9. Class 33s hauled most trains on the route between 1971 and 1980, thereafter mainly being limited to the weekend trains to and from Brighton. No.33025 is returning to that town on 30th March 1989 and is framed by the gantry over the connection from Yeovil Pen Mill. (P.G.Barnes)

10. Both running lines are signalled for reversible running, which is of particular value when Paddington-West of England services are diverted from their normal Taunton route. Trains from Waterloo then terminate at platform 2 (right), as seen on 30th March 1985. On the left, no. 50017 waits to leave for Penzance, while on the extreme right are the former down platform buildings used by engineering staff. (P.G.Barnes)

11. The civil engineers retain the use of some sidings and also the turntable for turning machines. Some steam specials were run from Salisbury at weekends in 1986-88, when the table was put to its intended use again. No.35028 *Clan Line* faces the former dual gauge transfer shed on 12th October 1986. (M.Turvey)

12. A 1990 view shows that the footbridge was shortened following closure of the down island platform - its offices can be seen through the bridge. The booking office was (and still is) on the platform. New wires can be added to the modern telephone pole without climbing it - they are simply pushed up its hollow interior. (J.Scrace)

SUTTON BINGHAM

13. An up train descends the 1 in 140 gradient and approaches the west crossover, presumably preparing to stop as staff are waiting on the platform. (Lens of Sutton)

The 1903 survey marks the three short sidings in the goods yard.

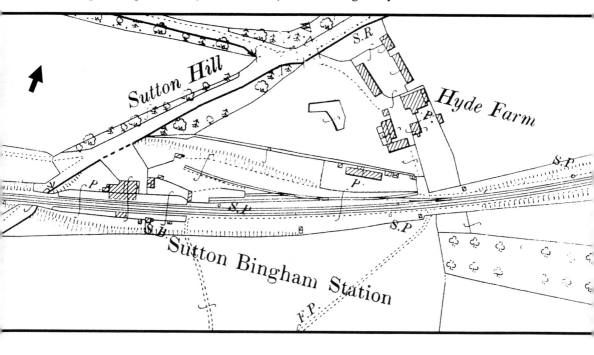

14. An SR sign was still carried on the north elevation ten years after nationalisation. Note the fine topiary silhouetted against Sutton Bingham reservoir. Although opened with the line, the station differs architecturally from its contemporaries. (R.M.Casserley)

15. By 1958 the canopies had gone and flat bottom rail had replaced the bull-head. The station became a halt on 1st August 1960 and closed on 31st December 1962. The final timetable showed six down and five up trains, weekdays only. (R.M.Casserley)

16. No.34070 *Manston*, another preserved Bulleid Pacific, speeds past the dock on 3rd May 1962, goods traffic having ceased on 4th April of that year. The centre siding had long gone. (C.L.Caddy)

17. Photographed on 10th April 1965, the signal box had ceased to function on 14th February of that year. Soon, little would remain of this lightly used station, the first on the route in Somerset. Yeovil Junction is a few yards into Dorset. (C.L.Caddy)

Hardington Sidings were three miles west of Sutton Bingham and were in public use from 8th January 1909 until 7th February 1937. The signal box (S.B.) closed in about 1959.

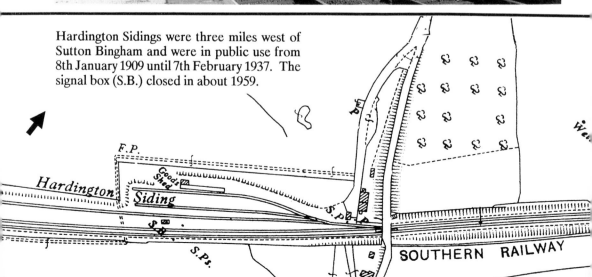

CREWKERNE

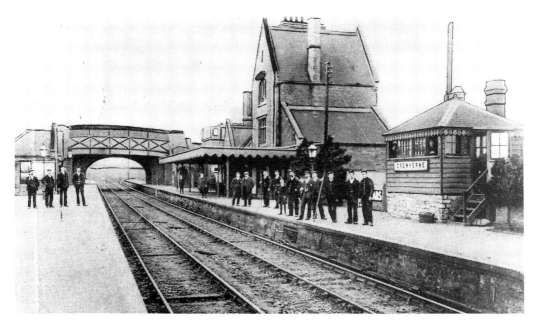

18. The station opened with the line and for its first 100 years served an almost static population of about 4500. Over a mile from the town centre, it is close to the village of Misterton. The small 12-lever signal box was superseded on 6th November 1960.
(Lens of Sutton)

19. The horse bus waiting to leave for the town must have been a welcome sight for a weary rail traveller from London. Apart from shortening of the canopy, this view is little altered today, although the water tank has been replaced by a pitched roof and the building let to Les Anstey & Sons.
(Lens of Sutton)

20. On 24th April 1953, no.35020 *Bibby Line* was travelling at about 70mph with the ten coaches of the 4.30pm Exeter Central to Waterloo when its crank axle broke. Mis- leading reports were made of the canopy collapsing due to the locomotive lurching or shedding its crank pin.   The official report stated that a flying brake block hit the cast iron

stanchion. (The other hit the bridge abutment). Steam from the crippled locomotive is visible in the distance, as the unlucky (but lucky to be alive) passengers wait for the stopping train (which was due at 6.9pm but arrived at 7.15), single line working having been instituted between Chard Junction and Sutton Bingham. (W.S.Rendell)

21.   All 30 locomotives of this class were withdrawn for examination and seven were found to have defective axles. Miraculously, no other wheels were derailed but ¾ mile of track was damaged.   Normal working was resumed at 9am on the next day.
(W.S.Rendell)

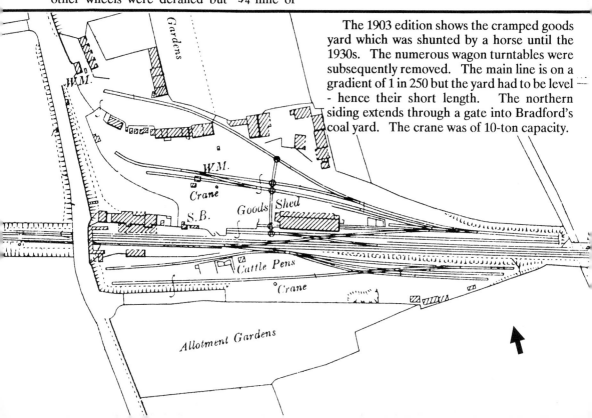

The 1903 edition shows the cramped goods yard which was shunted by a horse until the 1930s. The numerous wagon turntables were subsequently removed. The main line is on a gradient of 1 in 250 but the yard had to be level -- hence their short length.   The northern siding extends through a gate into Bradford's coal yard. The crane was of 10-ton capacity.

22. The new portion of canopy is evident below the 1859 builder's stone, as no.50018 *Resolution* arrives with the 13.15 from Waterloo on 10th August 1990. Next to the second coach is the 1960 signal box which had 24 levers and was in use until 26th February 1967, subsequently being used by the Permanent Way Dept. Closure of the goods yard took place on 18th April 1966 and the down platform on 7th May 1967. (C.Wilson)

23. The impressive structure is seen in July 1990, not long after major renovation work, which included stone cleaning. Courteous staff provide booking and Red Star parcel facilities. The station master once occupied the three-storey part but his garden was north of the goods shed. (J.Scrace)

WEST OF CREWKERNE

24. Fitted with automatic half barriers in November 1967, the level crossing at Crewkerne Gates is over ½ mile west of the station, the 205yd long Crewkerne Tunnel following in a further ½ mile. Class L11 no.E154 is seen emerging from it on 2nd August 1928. (H.C.Casserley)

0001

SOUTHERN RAILWAY
EVENING CHEAP
Available as advertised
Seaton to
CREWKERNE
Via Seaton Junc.
First Class

CONDITION BACK

SOUTHERN RAILWAY.
EVENING CHEAP
Available as advertised
Crewkerne
Seaton
Crewkerne to
SEATON
Via Seaton Junc
First Class
0001

SOUTHERN RLY.
PRIVILEGE TICKET
Available for One Week
including day of issue
BROAD CLYST to
Sutton
Via Bingham
FIRST CLASS
0039

25.   After nearly three miles of climbing at 1 in 80, almost continuously, down trains breasted the summit and were soon descending over Hewish Crossing. "King Arthur" class *The Green Knight* is doing so on 2nd August 1928.   The signal box was in use until 1967 when crossing lights were installed. These were replaced by AHBs in 1972. (H.C.Casserley)

A siding was available for public use from April 1900 until November 1963.   As a wartime measure, a loop was added on the down side in October 1942, it remaining usable until May 1967.

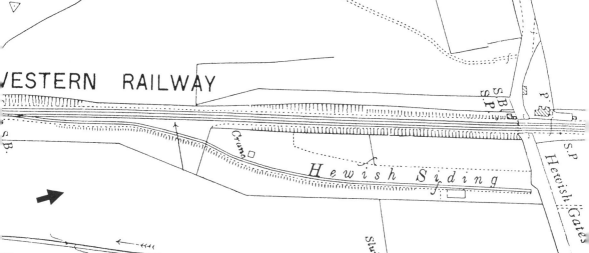

CHARD JUNCTION

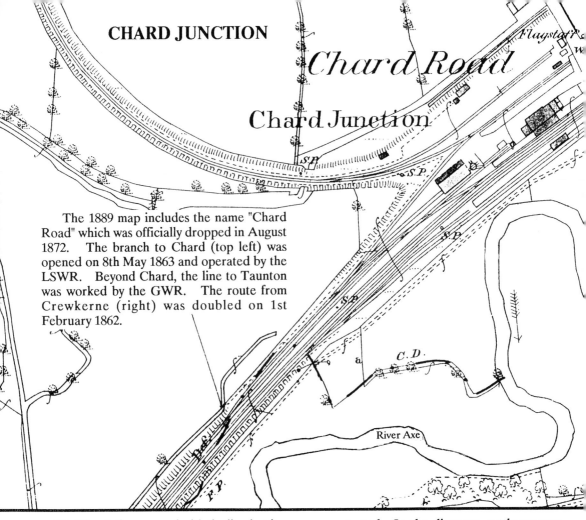

The 1889 map includes the name "Chard Road" which was officially dropped in August 1872. The branch to Chard (top left) was opened on 8th May 1863 and operated by the LSWR. Beyond Chard, the line to Taunton was worked by the GWR. The route from Crewkerne (right) was doubled on 1st February 1862.

26. The station opened with the line but it was many years before a footbridge was provided. Although this was covered, passengers for the branch train had to cross the station yard unprotected. In the distance, cattle wagons and horse boxes stand alongside the goods shed. (Author's coll)

27. Cattle wagons flank the up platform while vans stand coupled to a locomotive adjacent to the cast iron structure on the down platform which was of great value to gentlemen in the pre-corridor train era. (Lens of Sutton)

28. GWR no.632 rounds the final curve on the Chard branch as it approaches Chard Junction on 2nd August 1928. As a wartime economy measure it was arranged that the GWR would work the entire branch from 1st January 1917. Only occasionally, such as on summer Sundays in 1938, did the SR work trains to Chard. It was convenient for the railways and passengers alike for the entire line to Taunton to be worked as one. Chard became Chard Central in 1949 and on 2nd April 1950 the line from there to Thornfalcon was transferred to the Southern Region but existing operating methods continued. The route to Taunton closed to passengers on 10th September 1962. (H.C.Casserley)

29. No.34052 *Lord Dowding* rattles over the crossover as it rushes through with the 11.45am Waterloo to Plymouth train on 14th September 1957. On the left is the Chard Road Hotel, still retaining the pre-1872 name for the station. The gates were replaced by barriers on 14th January 1968. These were controlled from the signal box which was retained to work the passing loop. It has subsequently been rebuilt. (J.N.Faulkner)

30. The Wilts United Dairies established works south of the line and new sidings were provided to them in April 1937. The view shows the down side accommodation in about 1960. (Lens of Sutton)

31. A Taunton train waits to leave the branch platform on 28th April 1962, the small signal box having been demoted to a ground frame in March 1935. There was never a direct connection to the main line, a shunt always being necessary. On the left is the run-round loop and Bradford's siding. (E.Wilmshurst)

32. The footbridge had lost its cladding by the time this photograph was taken on 11th July 1964. It includes the cattle pens and no. 35006 *Peninsular & Oriental S.N.Co* heading the 11.45am from Waterloo to Ilfracombe, a Saturdays only express running non-stop between Templecombe and Sidmouth Junction. (E.Wilmshurst)

33. Pictured on the same day no. 34036 *Westward Ho* heads the 1.10pm Exeter Central to Chard Junction. It was scheduled to wait in the siding from 2.17 until 2.56 while two up expresses passed. It then continued to Yeovil Town. Also featured is the United Dairies petrol engined shunter. In recent years, only an occasional block train of tankers has used these sidings. (E.Wilmshurst)

34. Passenger services ceased on 7th March 1966 and freight facilities followed on 18th April of that year. The up side buildings and the goods shed survived into the 1980s but now not a brick remains. (C.Hall)

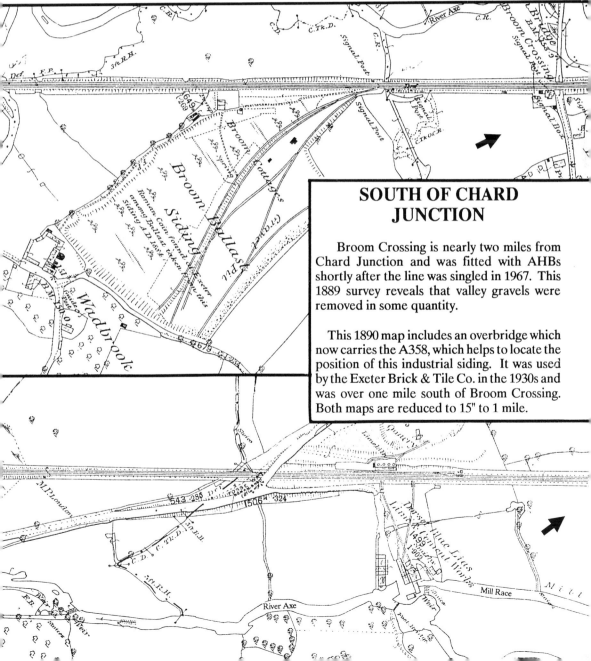

SOUTH OF CHARD JUNCTION

Broom Crossing is nearly two miles from Chard Junction and was fitted with AHBs shortly after the line was singled in 1967. This 1889 survey reveals that valley gravels were removed in some quantity.

This 1890 map includes an overbridge which now carries the A358, which helps to locate the position of this industrial siding. It was used by the Exeter Brick & Tile Co. in the 1930s and was over one mile south of Broom Crossing. Both maps are reduced to 15" to 1 mile.

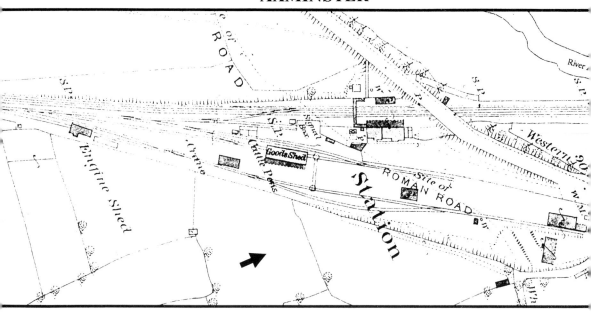

The 1st edition of 1889 shows a goods yard layout which changed little during its life. The engine shed housed a locomotive used for banking trains to Honiton but was demolished in about 1903 by which time the development of more powerful machines rendered this unnecessary.

35. As at Crewkerne, a prestigious station was erected when the line opened, although the population of the nearby town was then under 3000. Note that Bradfords were coal merchants here as well as at other stations on the route. Junction status was achieved when the Lyme Regis branch came into use on 24th August 1903. The tall chimneys and steeply pitched multiple gables were features widely employed by the architect, Sir William Tite. Mock Gothic seems in harmony with the pastoral area. (Lens of Sutton)

36. Even the buffers were clean as no. 768 *Sir Balin* arrived from London with carriages bearing roof boards listing the important stops.

37. A high standard of cleanliness was evident on 25th May 1935 as the driver oiled up prior to departure for Lyme Regis from the bay platform. Built in 1885, nos. 3125 and 3520

A goods train pauses at the up platform during shunting operations, sometime in the 1930s. (R.S.Carpenter coll.)

continued to work the branch until 1961. Except on Saturdays, only one engine was required. (H.C.Casserley)

38.   The 2.50 pm Waterloo to Ilfracombe passes at speed on 18th June 1949, headed by no. 35021 *New Zealand Line*.   It was at precisely this location that your author (V.M.) gasped at the first of these unique looking locomotives (no. 21C1) in 1941. (S.C.Nash)

39.   For several decades, there were three through freight trains to and from Exmouth Junction daily.   One such up service approaches the platforms on 8th July 1949, hauled by no. 449 *Sir Torre*.   The Axminster Carpet factory (left) had been re-established in 1937 and generated considerable rail traffic. (H.C.Casserley)

40. The other side of this bridge is seen in the background of the previous picture. It carried the Lyme Regis branch which descended at 1 in 80 to the bay platform. Class S15 no. 30827 accelerates the 10.0am Salisbury to Exeter Central stopping service on 6th September 1953. The abutments were still standing in 1991. (S.C.Nash)

Summary of Principal Services-

WATERLOO & SALISBURY, LYME REGIS, SEATON, SIDMOUTH, EXMOUTH, OKEHAMPTON, TAVISTOCK, DEVONPORT

DOWN									
		R		**R**		**P**	**R**	**R**	**R**
	a.m.	a.m.		a.m.		noon	p.m.	p.m.	p.m.
WATERLOO ....dep	1A 25	9A 0		11A 0		12P 0	1A 0	3A 0	6A 0	...
Salisbury..........................arr.	3 11	10 50	"ATLANTIC COAST EXPRESS"	12 23	"DEVON BELLE" FRIDAYS ONLY		2 39	4 42	7 44	...
Lyme Regis........................... ,,	8 56	12 54		3 11			5B 4	7 11	10Y 11	...
Seaton................................ ,,	8 17	12 51		3B27			5 3	7 9	9FO57	...
Sidmouth............................. ,,	8 27	1 22		2B27		3 43	5 32	6 48	10 10	...
Exmouth (via Tipton St. John's) ,,	...	1 45		2B51			...	7 12	10FO35	...
Exmouth (via Exeter Central)... ,,	7 10	...		2 43		4 26	5 11	...	10 43	...
Okehampton .... ,,	5 55	2 9		3 0			5 39	7 34	10 55	...
Tavistock North..................... ,,	6 29	2 39		3 39			6 17	8 7	11 23	...
Devonport King's Rd. .... ,,	7 31	3 10		4 6			6 48	8 34	11 52	...

MONDAYS TO FRIDAYS

A—Seats may be reserved at a fee of 1/- per seat, upon personal or postal request to the Station Master. Early application is advisable.   B—Through carriages from Waterloo. Y—By Southern National Omnibus between Axminster and Lyme Regis. Times subject to alteration.   FO—Fridays only

Summer 1953.
For weekend times, see under picture 81.

41. The 12.5pm from Lyme Regis arrives behind 4-4-2T no. 30583 (now on the Bluebell Railway) on 23rd Auguat 1951. The next train from the branch carried through coaches to

Waterloo which would be removed by T9 class no. 30336 (waiting between the signals) and attached to the rear of the next train to London. (N.Sprinks)

42. Water was pumped from the River Axe into the tank on the right, from where it was piped to three columns - one each end of the main platforms and one by the branch buffers. This busy scene was recorded on 9th June 1954. (S.W.Baker)

43. On 27th August 1960, no. 30582 (formerly SR no. 3125) was responsible for transferring coaches from the 3.5pm from Lyme Regis onto the rear of the 12.45pm from Torrington. The crane on the right was rated at 4ton 11cwt and ceased to be required when the goods traffic ceased on 18th April 1966. (J.H.Aston)

44. Following the demise of steam, local and branch line services were entrusted to DMUs. On 7th August 1965 the Lyme Regis service was worked by a 2- car class 118 unit while the 16.30 Yeovil Junction to Exeter Central service was formed of a Derby 3-car set. The branch closed on 29th November 1965 and the signal box followed on 5th March 1967. (J.N.Faulkner)

> **Other details about Axminster and 120 photographs of the branch are contained in our** *Branch Line to Lyme Regis.*

45. Singling was effective from 11th June 1967 and chimney stack shortening followed. Since 1973 the barriers at Axminster Gates, ½ mile north of the station, have been supervised by CCTV from the station - an unusual arrangement. (J.Scrace)

SEATON JUNCTION

46. The station opened with the line and was named "Colyton for Seaton" until the branch opened on 16th March 1868, when it became "Colyton Junction" and is seen here in its original form, looking westwards. (Lens of Sutton)

The initial track arrangements are shown on the 1904 edition. The hotel dates from 1898.

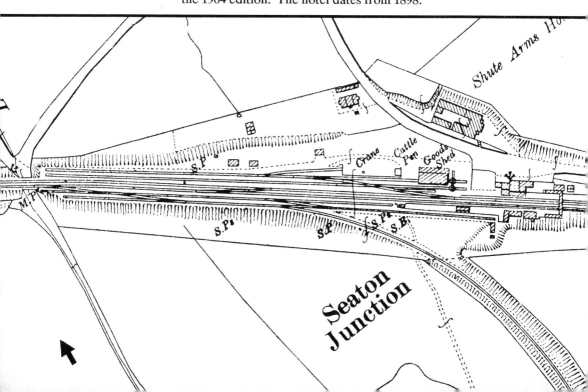

47. The station was extensively rebuilt in 1927-28 to give two through lines. The original offices were retained and new longer platforms built. (Lens of Sutton)

48. "King Arthur" class N15 no. 455 calls with an up stopping service while branch line stock stands in the distant siding. Lack of white platform edging indicates that this photograph was taken prior to 1936. (Lens of Sutton)

49. An up through freight passes the local goods yard on 17th June 1949. The train is headed by class S15 no. 30847, while class N15 no. 30455 *Sir Launcelot* waits with the 12.46 Salisbury to Exeter Central. The signal box came into use on 3rd April 1928. (S.C.Nash)

50. The shadows lengthen as no. 34054 *Lord Beaverbrook* disturbs the rural scene on 25th May 1963. It is arriving with the 3.5pm stopping train from Salisbury. Lower quadrant signals abound. (J.H.Aston)

51. The Seaton branch service was operated by class M7 0-4-4Ts for many decades, no. 30046 being typical. It is standing under the remarkably long footbridge provided in 1928 for a public footpath. The inter-platform bridge is on the left. (Lens of Sutton)

52. By 26th October 1963, at least three signals had been modernised with upper quadrants. No. 34030 *Watersmeet* leaves with the 12.36pm all-stations Salisbury to Exeter Central at 2.37pm. By then ex-GWR 0-6-0PTs had been introduced to the branch - no. 6412 is on the right. (E.Wilmshurst)

53. The new branch platform came into use on 13th February 1927, trains previously having had to reverse into the down bay. The branch and the station closed on 7th March 1966. The goods yard ceased to handle general traffic on 18th April of that year but coal continued to arrive until 8th May 1967 and milk was despatched for a few weeks longer. (C.L.Caddy)

54. A siding into the up platform was retained for some years but had gone when no. 50045 *Achilles* was photographed on 10th August 1990. The buildings were then occupied by four different businesses and both footbridges were still standing. (C.Wilson)

55. The climb between the Axe and Otter Valleys involved nearly eight miles of hard work, mostly at 1 in 80 - for engine and firemen in steam days. No. 50017 *Royal Oak* roars up with the 06.52 from Waterloo on 10th August 1990, while many passenger enjoy the scenery. (D.Brown)

Honiton Incline siding.—The points in the running line are operated by a spring lever, stand normally for the siding, and are trailing for down trains. Guards must see that all points are in correct position before moving trains into and out of the siding, and great care must be exercised by Enginemen not to stop their trains on the points leading into the siding, and to avoid a rebound of their train such as would be likely to cause the vehicles to take two roads at the points and become derailed. During the time Honiton Incline signal box is switched out no train can be shunted into the siding.

Honiton incline signal box was a block post one mile east of the tunnel and controlled a crossover. The down refuge siding point was a catch point, to divert any runaways into a siding. The box closed on 6th March 1966. Hydraulic rams were water powered water pumps requiring no outside energy source.

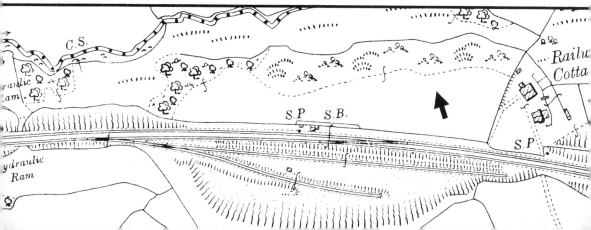

56. The western portal of the 1345yd long Honiton Tunnel is at the summit of the incline. No. 34089 *602 Squadron* emerges from it on 5th September 1964 with the 10.35am Waterloo to Padstow. The tunnel was the longest on the LSWR. (S.C.Nash)

57. On 14th August 1966, LNER designed class A2 no. 60532 *Blue Peter* stalled while climbing Honiton Bank - a sad sight within months of the end of steam in the South of England. The tour was from Waterloo via Exeter, Taunton, Westbury and back to Waterloo. (S.C.Nash)

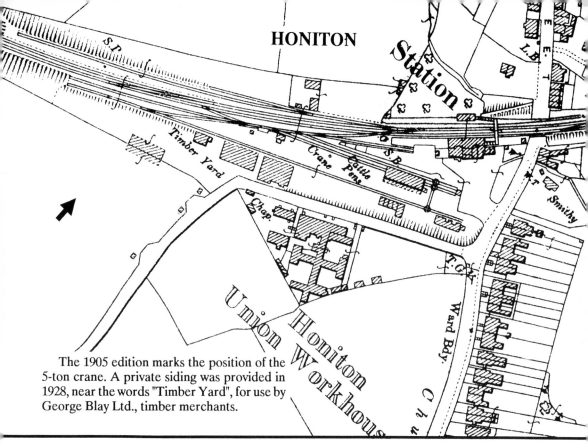

HONITON

The 1905 edition marks the position of the 5-ton crane. A private siding was provided in 1928, near the words "Timber Yard", for use by George Blay Ltd., timber merchants.

58. Of similar architectural style to Crewkerne and Axminster, the fine building was on the south side of the line, remote from the town. New Street (right) passes under the railway and runs to the town centre, less than ½ mile distant. (Lens of Sutton)

59. As at Chard Junction, there were few through trains to Waterloo until 1964, a change at Salisbury being necessary, except in the early years. Milk churns, however, were given a prompt and direct service to the Metropolis. Empty churns stand on the right. (D.Cullum coll.)

60. The hipped-roof waiting shelter was similar to those at the other original stations on the route but the ornate down canopy valance was one of the few to remain. The 10.15am express for the West of England dashes down the steep gradient on 11th July 1964, headed by no. 35010 *Blue Star*. The incline eased to 1 in 300 through the platforms. (E.Wilmshurst)

61. The 1967 singling scheme involved the provision of a passing loop and an up refuge siding here. The latter can be seen by the 1957 signal box. The down track is signalled for bi-directional running, as illustrated by the arrival of the 16.22 Exeter St. Davids to Waterloo at the down platform on 25th July 1990. The locomotive is no. 50024 *Vanguard*. (J.Scrace)

62. Goods traffic ceased on 8th May 1967 and the station was rebuilt using the featureless CLASP system. Enough said. (D.Brown)

63. Class 158 air-conditioned units nos. 158732/7 appeared on 15th October 1990 on a special working from Waterloo. Similar class 159 units were expected to be introduced into traffic in May 1992 which would give new standards of comfort, provided more legroom has been given than in their predecessors. (D.Wilson)

The 1926 revision of the 1" to 1 mile map marks a halt 1/2 mile west of Honiton station. This was Round Ball Halt, opened on 29th September 1906 for the benefit of Territorials using the nearby rifle range. It was a request stop and seems not to have been used after 1914. The location of the tunnel is also shown.

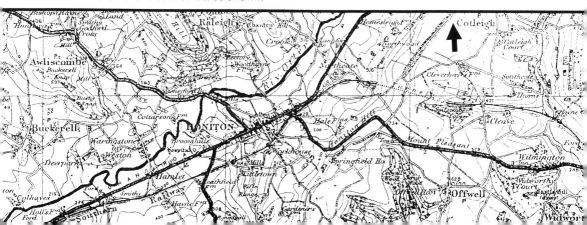

SIDMOUTH JUNCTION

64. This westward view includes the now familiar station house and offices of Tite's design. Opened as "Feniton", the name was changed to "Ottery Road" in July 1861, to "Ottery St. Mary" in April 1868 and to "Sidmouth Junction" on 6th July 1874, when the branch opened. (Lens of Sutton)

The 1905 survey shows the Sidmouth branch lower right. Above it are two sidings parallel to the main line from Honiton. When opened, the station served Feniton (1 mile - pop. 360) and Ottery St. Mary (3 miles - pop. 4400).

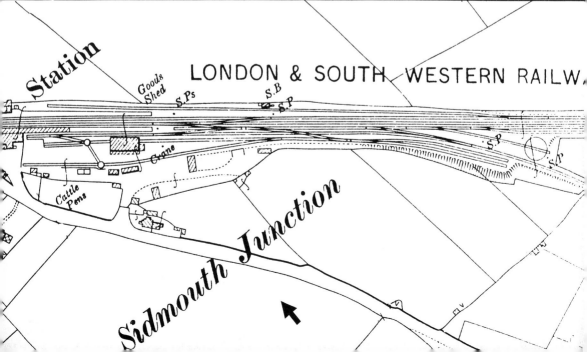

65. On 4th August 1928, class S15 no. E831 was
standing at the down platform during shunting
operations. Traffic figures for that year are as
follows (1936 figures in brackets) - tickets
issued 21,000 (13,000); tickets collected 22,000
(16,000); telegrams 6000 (3000); tons of solid
fuel received 880 (1200); general goods
received 3250 tons (2000) and despatched 540
(490). Lavatory receipts increased from £2 to
£6 and the peak year for milk traffic was 1932,
when 116,000 cans were despatched.
(H.C.Casserley)

66. A 1938 westward view from the road
bridge show the Sidmouth branch curving to
the left. The turntable was situated to the right
of the permanent way hut many years previously. (J.R.W.Kirkby)

67. The gate box is in its original position. It was later moved south of the track and fitted with five levers, working the gate locks and the nearby crossover. It remained in use until 23rd June 1974, although the line between Honiton and Pinhoe was singled on 11th June 1967. (Lens of Sutton)

68. The signal box contained 31 levers and was in use until 21st May 1967. Note that the down platform was signalled for the starting of the through London trains to and from the branch. No. 35025 *Brocklebank Line* blows off as she departs for London on 31st May 1963. (J.H.Aston)

69. As the original "Merchant Navy" locomotive, no. 35001 *Channel Packet,* arrives on 17th August 1963, we can see the revised position of the gate box. The engine had been rebuilt from its original form by then. The train is the 11.48am from Plymouth, which was booked to stop here from 2.48 to 2.53 and to reach Waterloo at 6.19pm. (J.N.Faulkner)

70. The 5-ton crane is evident as congestion demands that the branch line coaches are stabled on the goods shed road. The locomotives are BR class 3 2-6-2T no. 82018 and

"Merchant Navy" class no. 35026 *Lamport & Holt Line*. The latter is working the 10.30am Exeter Central to Waterloo on 6th July 1961. (R.C.Riley)

71. Having traversed the distant hills in the vicinity of Honiton, a "Warship" arrives, bound for Exeter. These powerful machines were introduced in 1964 but were displaced by the lower rated class 33s in 1971. Containers stand on flat wagons in the yard. (Lens of Sutton)

FENITON

72. Sidmouth Junction remained open until 6th March 1967, when the branch closed completely, and the buildings were subsequently destroyed. However, local pressure and increased housing development led to the reopening of the station as "Feniton" on 3rd May 1971. The lone railman in the small gate box issued tickets until 1974, when an office was provided on the platform, the barriers being controlled from there. No.50046 *Ajax* is westbound on 4th February 1991. (M.Turvey)

WHIMPLE

73. The main buildings were on the up side and date to the opening of the line. The rip saw tooth style of valance appears to be painted in two colours. This section of the LSWR was one of the most profitable for many years. (Lens of Sutton)

The 1905 map marks the cider (then spelt with a "y") factory established by Henry Whiteway & Co in 1892. Note that the corn mill is rail connected.

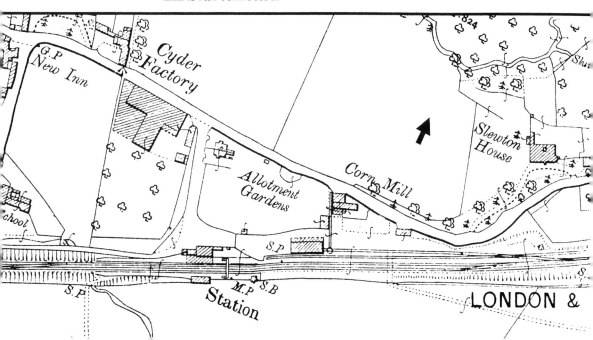

74. In 1903 Whiteways opened a bottling plant at Vauxhall and so the overnight goods service to Nine Elms was of great value to the firm. Here we witness the unloading of a new bottle washing machine in 1950. In 1989, production at Whimple ceased and was concentrated at Whitchurch, near Bristol. (E.V.M.Whiteway)

75. The 1967 singling resulted in all passengers using the down platform (left). The cross-overs were retained, with ground frames, as was 1/2 mile of the up line. This gave access to the goods yard which was closed to public traffic on 4th December 1967 but retained for use by Whiteways. Staffing ceased on 5th October 1970 but the hut by the steps on the left was available for ticket sales in the mornings. (P.G.Barnes)

76. This and the previous picture was taken on 6th July 1990 as the sidings and connections were being removed. No.50001 *Dreadnought* heads the 06.52 from Waterloo, one of only four down trains to stop here on weekdays, three in the early morning and one in the evening. Demolition of the goods shed took place in 1991, the year in which BR withdrew wagonload service and the Government decided that railborne freight should be doubled. In the 1930s Whiteways despatched about 30,000 tons of their products annually by rail. Goods inward included coal, bottles, casks and apples. (P.G.Barnes)

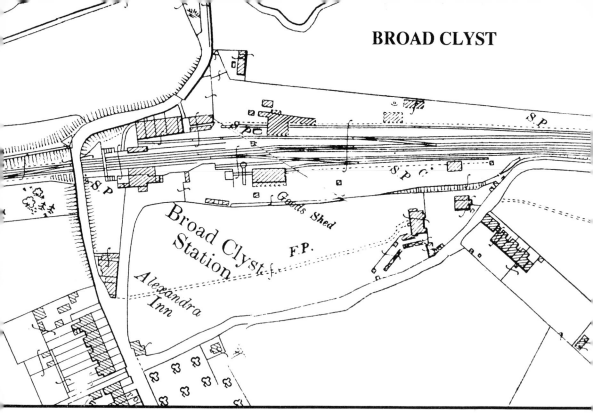

The 1905 edition marks one line in the engineer's yard unconnected to the others. This was presumably for movement of materials within the yard. The goods yard closed on 6th September 1965, having earlier despatched large quantities of locally grown sugar beet.

77. The village from which the station takes its name is over one mile to the north. For 100 years its population was 2000 to 2500 and, being on the A38, it had an adequate bus service from the 1920s. The standard station buildings of the route are evident, but four cottages were added by the LSWR, on the right. (Lens of Sutton)

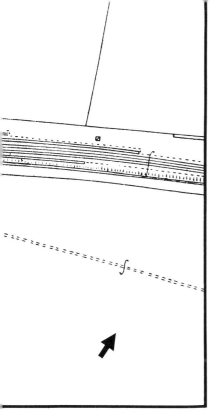

78.   Goods shunting is in progress as we look
east from the road bridge. The Civil Engineer
established a yard on the left in 1896 and
expanded it in 1926, as seen. The goods yard
and shed are on the right.   (Lens of Sutton)

79. Permanent way materials stand in the up yard as class H15 no. 30330 drifts in with the 3.36pm Templecombe to Exeter Central stopping train on 16th June 1949. Ageing compartment stock is much in evidence. (S.C.Nash)

80. The engineer's shunter on 24th May 1957 was no. 49S, a petrol engined device. The up starting signals and the signal box are included in this picture. The depot closed at the end of 1964. (T.Wright)

81. The south elevation presented a smart appearance in July 1959. It did likewise in 1990, although devoid of the single storey area and occupied by estate agents. The last passengers used the station on 7th March 1966. (R.M.Casserley)

DOWN		RN		R				R	RM	P
	a.m.	a.m.	a.m.	a.m.	a.m.	a.m.	a.m.	a.m.	a.m.	noon
WATERLOO ....dep	1AD25	7A 33		8A 5	8A 54	9A 0	10 45	11A 15	11A 45	12P 0
Salisbury ....arr.	3 11	9 19		9 47	10 50	11 0	12 16	12 42	1 21	...
Lyme Regis .... ,,	8 53	...		11B 56	...	1 6	2B11	...	...	...
Seaton .... ,,	8 17	...		11B 37	...	1 10	2B 5	...	...	...
Sidmouth .... ,,	8 27	...		12B 6	...	1B 52	...	...	3B 26	3 43
Exmouth (via Tipton St. John's) ,,	...	...		12B 38	...	1B 58	...	...	3B 58	...
Exmouth (via Exeter Central)... ,,	7 10	12 9		...	...	...	...	3 19	...	4 11
Okehampton .... ,,	5 55	12 3		...	2 23	...	...	3 34	...	...
Tavistock North .... ,,	6 29	1 38		...	2 54	...	...	4 11	...	...
Devonport King's Rd............. ,,	7 31	2 16		...	3 25	...	...	4 38	...	...

(Columns annotated vertically: "Commencing 4th July" / "Commencing 4th July" ; "DEVON BELLE")

DOWN								"DEVON BELLE"	
	R		R		R	R	R	P	R
	p.m.	p.m.	p.m.	p.m.	p.m.	a.m.	a.m.	noon	p.m.
WATERLOO ....dep	1A 0	1 5	3A 0	3A 5	6A 0	11A 0	11A 5	12P 0	4A 0
Salisbury ....arr.	2 39	2 50	4 42	4 52	7 44	12 48	12 57	...	5 42
Lyme Regis .... ,,	...	5 4	...	7 11	10Y 11	...	2 44	...	7 39
Seaton .... ,,	...	5 3	...	7 10	9 57	...	2 40	...	7 37
Sidmouth .... ,,	...	5 38	6 50	...	10 10	2 50	...	3 43	8 12
Exmouth (via Tipton St. John's) ,,	...	6 1	7 15	...	10 35	3 15	...	...	8 34
Exmouth (via Exeter Central)... ,,	5 11	...	...	...	...	...	...	4 11	...
Okehampton .... ,,	5 39	...	7 34	...	10 59	3 45	...	...	9 9
Tavistock North............ ,,	6 17	...	8 7	...	11 26	4 15	...	...	9 48
Devonport King's Rd............. ,,	6 48	...	8 34	...	11 56	4 44	...	...	10 21

(SATURDAYS—continued | SUNDAYS ; Sunday "DEVON BELLE" column annotated "To 13th September only")

A—Seats may be reserved at a fee of 1/- per seat, upon personal or postal request to the Station Master. Early application is advisable. B—Through carriages from Waterloo. D—Departs 1.35 a.m. until 29th August. FO—Fridays only P—1st and 3rd Class Pullman Cars only between Waterloo, Sidmouth Junction, Exeter Central. Limited bookings. Supplementary fees—1st Class, 7s. 0d. ; 3rd Class, 4s. 0d. Reservations CANNOT be booked by telephone. Application, with fee, to be made to the Station Master. R—Refreshment car between Waterloo and Exeter. RM—Refreshment Car between Waterloo and Exmouth. RN—Refreshment Car between Waterloo and Okehampton.

Summer 1953

82. No. 34100 *Appledore* heads an up freight on 12th September 1964, while invalid cars stand on LOWFITs on the left. These three-wheeled vehicles were manufactured locally and loaded in large quantities that year. The signal box had 14 levers and was in use until 12th December 1965, although open only as necessary in its last year. The down line was retained after singling in June 1967. (C.L.Caddy)

83. On the same day, a Yeovil Junction - Exeter Central train departs, next stop Pinhoe. The railway cottages on the right are unusual in having been built on massive brick arches. This may been due to poor ground conditions or to the frequent flooding of the Clyst Valley hereabouts, the road north having special provisions for floods. (C.L.Caddy)

84. In 1959, the engineer's yard shunter was replaced by diesel engine no. DS1169, which had earlier been employed on coast defence work at Folkestone Warren. (C.L.Caddy)

PINHOE

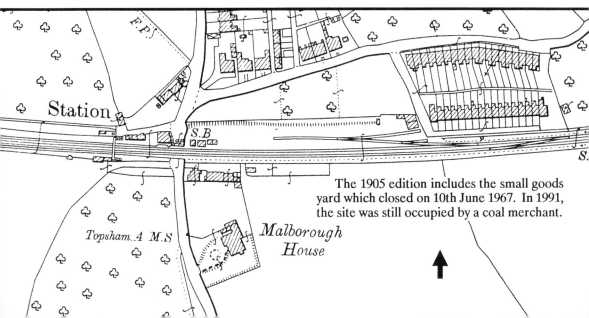

The 1905 edition includes the small goods
yard which closed on 10th June 1967. In 1991,
the site was still occupied by a coal merchant.

85. Opened more than ten years after the line (on 30th October 1871), this was one of the few stations to have non-standard buildings. Only three miles from Exeter, the station is situated conveniently to the village. (D.Cullum)

87. A 1990 eastward view shows the platforms restored, the station having reopened on 16th May 1983. The single line to Honiton commences in the distance. In the summer of 1991 there were weekday departures for Exeter St. Davids at 07.30, 08.15, 10.30 and 18.33. Up trains called at 06.26. 17.48 and 19.49. (J.Scrace)

86. Looking towards Exeter on 8th July 1959, we see the crossing keeper's house, which is now privately occupied. The footbridge and platform buildings were removed after the station closed on 7th March 1966. Half barriers supervised from the signal box were installed on 17th March 1968, the box closing in February 1988. (R.M.Casserley)

Diagram of the private sidings between Pinhoe (right) and Whipton Bridge Halt. The halt was in use between March 1906 and January 1923.

A. Grain Silo sidings.

B. Poltimore Brick Co. siding - in use until 6th September 1965.

C. Goverment Food Store siding usable between 1942 and 1969. Reopened to serve Continental (London) Ltd. until 1979.

D. Pye Storage Ltd sidings from September 1953 until March 1968.

E. Crossover removed in May 1967.

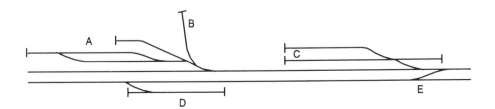

L. & S. W. R.

YEOVIL & EXETER BRANCH

Stone

S.P

Exmouth Junction

S.Box

The new engine shed came into use on 3rd November 1887 and is shown on the 1st edition. At the lower border is the branch to Exmouth and on the left are buildings used by the signal and permanent way engineers. The turntable was 55ft. long and north of the shed can be seen two elevated coaling stages.

88. The shed was constructed with light steel components and clad with corrugated iron sheets. All this was subject to rapid corrosion and by 1900 the structure was in poor condition. By the time this photograph was taken on 18th July 1925, work had started on the construction of a new shed, east of the old one. The first task was the removal of the turntable - a new 65ft. one was installed in the south-east corner of the site. (H.C.Casserley)

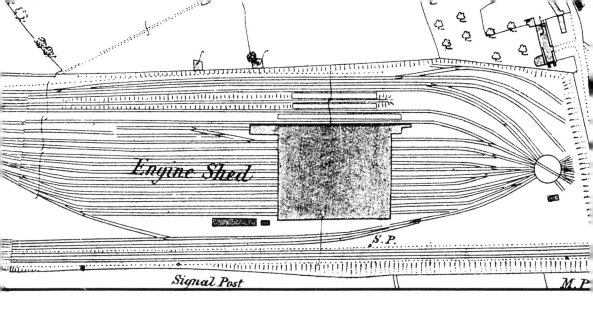

Engine Shed

Signal Post

S.P.

M.P.

89. The shed was built from concrete components cast at the company's works on the north-west part of the site. The building was largely complete by 1927 and is seen in April 1938, in the company of one of the popular N class, which is standing on the turntable road. (H.N.James coll.)

SOUTHERN

1854

90. The coaling tower provided an excellent vantage point for this photograph on 29th June 1948. Top left are the offices, stores and workshops. The high roof accommodated a travelling gantry crane of 63 ton capacity, this allowing all but the heaviest repairs to be undertaken. (J.H.Aston)

91. Two "Pacifics" are seen here leaving the shed on 16th June 1949, bound for Exeter Central where they would take the two portions of the prestigious all- Pullman express westward. No. 34041 *Wilton* leads no. 34011 *Tavistock*, which is in the experimental light green livery. (S.C.Nash)

92. Exmouth Junction Box is viewed from the loco shed yard on 18th June 1926, as class G6 no. E267 carries out its shunting duties. It is attached to a special shunter's wagon. The box was replaced by the present one on 15th November 1959. (H.C.Casserley)

93. An eastbound local service headed by 0-4-4T class T1 no. 17 obscures the junction box on 3rd August 1928. Opened on 1st May 1861, the branch to Exmouth is unclear in the allotments on the left. The line beyond the left signal post connected with eight sidings of Down Yard. Almost all freight trains (upto 60 per day) terminated at Exmouth Junction for remarshalling. (H.C.Casserley)

94. The Exmouth lines are on the left as no. 35015 *Rotterdam Lloyd* lifts the twelve Pullman cars up the incline from Exeter Central on 24th June 1950. The unusual concrete towers carried power cables from the Corporation's electricity works to the locomotive depot. (J.J.Smith)

MOUNT PLEASANT ROAD HALT

95. The halt was opened on 26th January 1906, when railmotors were introduced on local services between Exeter Queen Street and Honiton. The steep path to the up platform is on the left of this view of a T9, blurred due to the slow shutter speeds of earlier days. The halt closed on 2nd January 1928.
(Lens of Sutton)

96. Access to the up platform of the halt was via the gateway in the foreground. This eastward view on 6th July 1990 has the branch signal to the right of the pole, which largely obscures the junction and the box. To the left and in the distance is the saw tooth outline of a Leo Supermarket, built on the site of the locomotive shed. The other buildings were still used by the civil engineers for plant maintenance. No.50029 *Renown* heads the 09.15 from Waterloo. (P.G.Barnes)

97. Western Fuels shunter and mechanised storage bins are seen in detail, early in 1991. Their coal concentration depot (on the left of the picture above) was built on the site of the former SR Concrete Works. (M.Turvey)

ST. JAMES PARK

98. After passing through the 263yd long Blackboy Tunnel, the line falls at 1 in 100 through St.James Park Halt, which was opened as Lions Holt Halt on 26th January 1906. The name was changed on 7th October 1946 and it was photographed looking towards London on 28th July 1962. (R.M.Casserley)

99. Exeter Central is in the distance as no.50046 *Ajax* climbs towards Exmouth Junction on 5th February 1991. At this time only the Exmouth branch trains stopped at St.James Park, much used when Exeter City is playing at home. (M.Turvey)

EXETER QUEEN STREET

100. A boot polisher kneels at the entrance to Northernhay, while a carter rests at the top of the down side station approach, the station being in the background. (Lens of Sutton)

101. Entering the station, passengers were confronted with smoke and gloom. As all trains to and from the west changed locomotives here, there were inevitably engines standing under the roof during the long stop for this purpose. (D.Cullum coll.)

102. There were two up and one down through roads. Originally there had been four, but "C" Box had been built at the far end of the station in about 1880, blocking the down through line, "B" Box being at the eastern approach.
(Lens of Sutton)

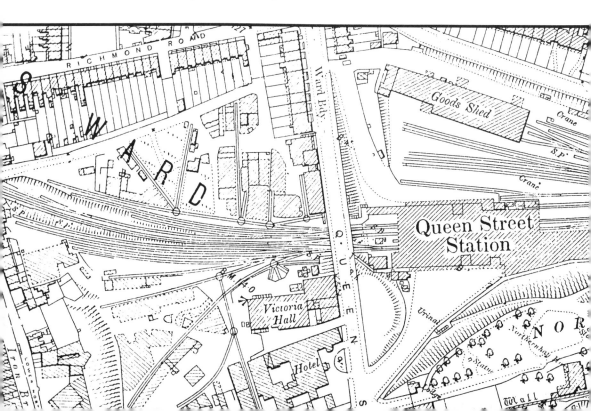

QUEEN St YARD. cvi.

103. On the left, stock stands on the site of the first locomotive depot. A ticket (collecting) platform had originally stood where the line of loaded coal wagons rest. White painted cattle pens are on the right. (Lens of Sutton)

The notable feature of the station on the 1905 map is that the entrances are on the north and south sides, not on the bridge, as now. Until 1887 part of the area between the two bridges on the right was occupied by the locomotive shed - it covered the three parallel tracks north of the turntable. The latter was derelict in 1905 and the area was used for locomotive servicing and coach berthing. The line to St.Davids enters a tunnel near the left margin.

104. "King Arthur" class no.E749 *Iseult* waits at the up platform for mail bags to be loaded on 3rd August 1928. In 1925 the up platform had been lengthened to accommodate two trains simultaneously - hence the signal in the middle of the platform. (H.C.Casserley)

105. An eastward view shows track and platform alterations in progress and a new signal post. By the bridge is "B" Box, which closed on 15th June 1927. (Lens of Sutton)

106. At the west end, the 1 in 37 gradient up from St.Davids presented a severe operational challenge with most trains in the steam era requiring assistance. Class G6 0-6-0T no.257 pilots class S11 4-4-0 no.401 on 18th June 1926. On the left some of the eight berthing sidings are visible. Up to 73 coaches could be berthed in the various sidings at this station. (H.C.Casserley)

EXETER CENTRAL

107. An almost total rebuild of the station was completed on 1st July 1933, the opening ceremony coinciding with celebrations to mark the 800th anniversary of the consecration of the first altar in Exeter Cathedral. A civic procession was held and the station was formally renamed. The ground floor included shops, divisional offices being established on the upper floors. The standards had earlier carried the tramways' overhead wire. (N.Langridge coll.)

Main line arrivals at Exeter Central in August 1934 (Mondays to Fridays)	
a.m.	From
4.39	Portsmouth & Southsea
8.12	Yeovil Town
8.50	Honiton
9.32	Templecombe
11.13	Sidmouth Junction
11.19	Salisbury
12.22	Salisbury
p.m.	
1.03	Waterloo
1.44	Seaton Junction
1.49	Waterloo (ACE)
2.22	Waterloo
2.48	Seaton Junction
3.24	Salisbury
4.05	Sidmouth Junction
4.22	Brighton
4.46	Waterloo
5.26	Seaton Junction
5.56	Honiton
6.2	Salisbury
6.23	Waterloo
6.56	Sidmouth Junction
7.22	Templecombe
7.29	Axminster
9.56	Sidmouth Junction
10.04	Waterloo
10.40	Templecombe
11.04	Honiton

108. The old footbridge was removed and a new additional entrance was provided from New North Road. It had its own booking office at the end of the new footbridge, both of which were closed as a wartime economy measure. *Salisbury* is seen on 31st August 1945. (H.C.Casserley)

→

110. The almost window-less "Tavern Cars" were introduced in 1949 and were of limited popularity. Like other catering vehicles, they were attached to and detached from London trains at Exeter Central. *The Green Man* is seen coupled to ex-LBSCR class E1/R 0-6-2T no.32135 on 17th September 1955. (T.Wright)

109. The retaining wall in the background was reputedly built in the moat of Exeter Castle. The 3.5pm stopping train from Salisbury has just arrived on 15th June 1950, behind class S15 no.30841, which is now resident on the North Yorkshire Moors Railway. (J.J.Smith)

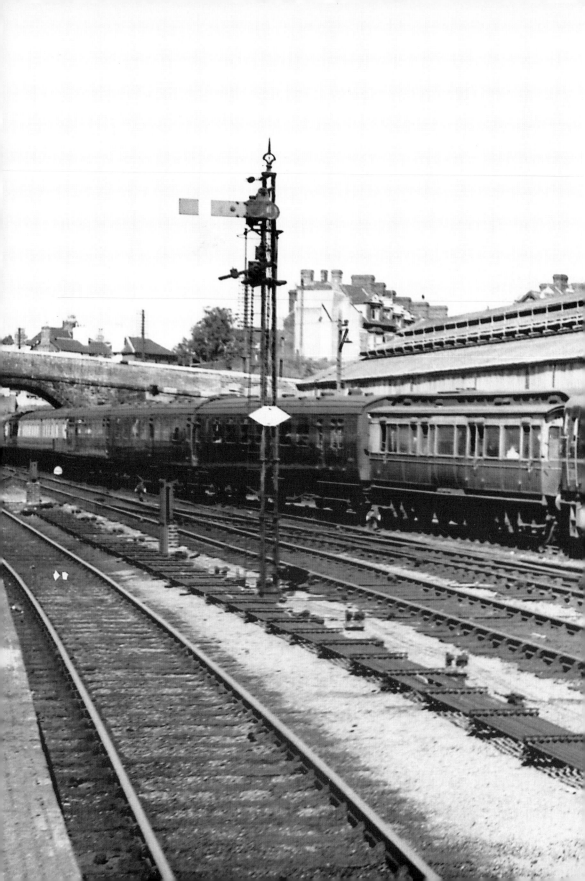

111. The 1930 carriage cleaning shed is in the background as 1-Co-Co-1 diesel-electric no.10203 arrives on test with a dynamometer car and the 1.0pm from Waterloo on 5th July 1955. Brighton built, this locomotive and its two sisters were in regular use on the route in the 1950s, often working two return trips daily. (E.W.Fry)

112. A look down the incline from Queen Street bridge in August 1956 shows that wagon turntables were still in place in the goods yard. Note the trap siding on the up line - there were two more beyond the 184yd long St.David's Tunnel to catch any runaways. (D.Cullum)

1934 Appendix

Horse dock sidings, up side cattle dock and Palmer and Sawdye's coal stores.—Bogie vehicles must not be permitted to pass into the horse dock on the down side at the St. David's end of Exeter Central or the up side cattle dock, neither must a passenger vehicle, van, horse box, or other covered vehicle pass alongside Messrs. Palmer & Sawdye's coal stores.

Traders' sidings.—The sidings serving the lettings of The East Devon Agricultural Co-Operative Society, Messrs. R. W. & F. C. Sharp, Messrs. Heywood and Sons, The Devon Trading Company, and Messrs. Bowden Bros., are connected with No. 2 up siding, west end, by means of turntables, and the working of the wagons to and from the sidings must be carried out in accordance with the following instructions:—

Wagons for the respective Traders must be placed in the Company's siding at convenient points near the turntables serving the appropriate sidings, and wagons from the Traders' sidings will be received at the same points.

The responsibility for the movement of wagons between the respective points of exchange and the Traders' sidings, including the operation of the turntables, rests with the respective firms, and when such movements are required to be made, application must be made by the Traders' men to the Shunter at Exeter Central " B " box, or other member of the station staff, who will make arrangements with the Signalman at Exeter Central " B " box for the turntables to be released at a convenient time to enable the work to be carried out.

Before any movement of wagons in the Company's sidings is made by the Traders' men, the Shunter or other member of the station staff, must place a red flag in a conspicuous position near the hand points controlling entrance to the sidings, which must be kept exhibited until the work has been completed, and the turntables have been replaced to their normal position and locked.

The movement of wagons over the turntables must be authorised by the Company's staff, who will be responsible for seeing that the turntables have been replaced to their original position after completion of the work, and advise the Signalman so that the turntables may be locked.

113. Steam envelops the Exmouth train at platform 4 on 29th September 1956. The locomotive is class M7 no.30669. The goods yard closed to general traffic on 4th December 1967. (H.C.Casserley)

114. Class E1/R no.31235 is seen again, having been turned. Recorded in September 1958, its train is mostly carrying containers, and stands adjacent to the cattle dock road. The carriage sidings on the right were removed in 1970. (Pamlin Prints)

115. Class Z 0-8-0T no.30951 is on the down through road on 13th October 1962. Most of this class came to Exeter in 1959, primarily for banking purposes. The less popular class W 2-6-4Ts arrived for this duty in 1962, to be followed by Western Region 0-6-0PTs in 1963. (A.E.Bennett)

116. No.34069 *Hawkinge* reaches the top of the incline on 21st September 1962 and passes the 35-lever Exeter "B" Box, which opened on 13th September 1925 and closed on 23rd February 1970. The maximum unassisted load for Bulleid Pacifics from St.Davids was 200 tons. (R.M.Casserley)

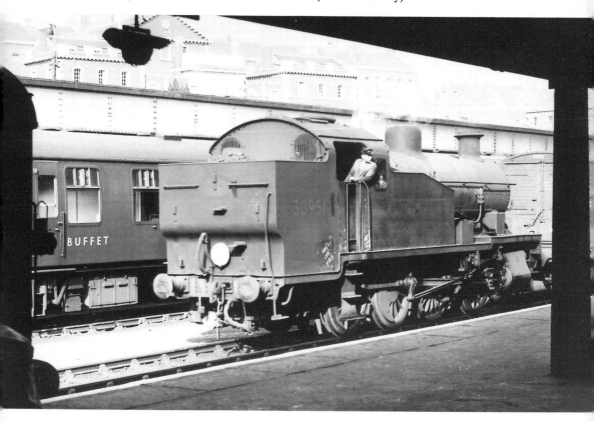

117. No.34107 *Blandford Forum* is standing near the scissors crossover, which was used when trains from the west were to be united for their journey to Waterloo. The first train to arrive would generally stop at the St.Davids end of the platform, the engine would be detached and then run out over the scissors, as the London-bound engine would be standing ready at the east of the platform. This would then reverse down onto the coaches and haul them to the far end of the platform. Another locomotive would be waiting on the up through line with the restaurant cars. These would be propelled over the scissors, onto the rear of the front portion. This locomotive would withdraw and the second train from the west would arrive. Its locomotive would run out over the crossover and the main train would then run back to couple onto the rear portion. The procedure applied to most up expresses, except the ACE, nineteen minutes being the normal allowance for the complete operation. (C.L.Caddy)

118. "A" Box became Exeter Central in 1970, its location being shown in picture no.114. It was in use until 6th May 1985 when its functions were taken over by a new panel at St. Davids. The box survives as an instruction room. (C.Hall)

119. The up through road was taken out of use on 9th November 1969 and the down through followed on 13th October 1984. The yard sidings remained in use as a cement terminal for Blue Circle until January 1990, tankers originating from Aberthaw and Westbury. No.50002 *Superb* waits to leave for Waterloo at 12.28 on 27th June 1990. (P.G.Barnes)

120. By 1990, the station had lost its forlorn look, plant tubs helping to fill the gap. The spacious booking hall had been lost to commerce but the Exmouth branch had gained a 30-minute interval service, three trains terminating in the bay platform (no.1) on weekdays, the others continuing to St.Davids or beyond. (J.Scrace)

MP Middleton Press

Easebourne Lane, Midhurst, West Sussex GU29 9AZ
Tel: (0730) 813169 Fax: (0730) 812601

Companion albums in this style for other West of England lines

Branch Lines ...
Branch Lines to Exmouth
Branch Line to Lyme Regis
Branch Line to Lynton
Branch Line to Minehead
Branch Lines to Seaton and Sidmouth
Branch Line to Swanage to 1992
Branch Lines around Weymouth
(Abbotsbury, Easton and The Quay Tramway)

Southern Main Lines ...
Exeter to Barnstaple
Salisbury to Yeovil
Yeovil to Exeter

Country Railway Routes ...
Bath to Evercreech Junction
Bournemouth to Evercreech Junction
Burnham to Evercreech Junction
Yeovil to Dorchester
(including the Bridport Branch)

Write or telephone for the full list of Southern Classics

ANNUAL 1999

PICTURES COURTESY OF LONDON TOURIST BOARD
WEBSITE www.LondonTown.com

£5.50
UK only

This book belongs to:

Contents

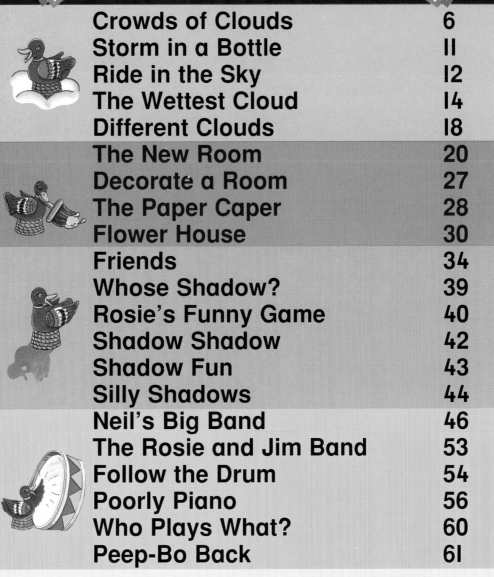

© 1998 Ragdoll Productions (UK) Ltd.
Design of the Rosie and Jim puppets and photographic dolls
copyright © Ragdoll Productions (UK) Ltd.
a Ragdoll Production for ITV. All Rights Reserved.
Published in Great Britain in 1998 by World International Ltd., Deanway Technology Centre,
Wilmslow Road, Handforth, Cheshire, SK9 3FB.
Printed in Italy. ISBN 0 7498 3771 3

written by Kjartan Poskitt
illustrated by Jane Swift

Crowds of Clouds

1. "Quack! Quack!" said Duck. "Gosh, Rosie!" said Jim. "What a lovely sunny day!" "Tootle has been washing his clothes!" said Rosie. "I'll hang them out to dry," said Neil.

2. "There!" said Neil. "They will soon be dry in the warm sunshine!" "Look what's coming across the sky!" said Rosie. "It's a big, black cloud!" said Jim.

3. "It's not sunny anymore!" said Rosie. "I feel a bit colder," said Jim. "I wonder where the sun has gone?" "The big cloud has covered it up, you noggin!" giggled Rosie.

4. "Oh no!" said Neil. "I think it's going to rain. I don't want my washing to get wetter!" "Tootle is taking his washing down again," laughed Jim.

6

5. "If it's going to rain, we'd better get ready!" said Rosie. "We can use this big cloth," said Jim. "You can be under the cloth too, Duck," said Rosie. "Quack!" said Duck.

6. "It doesn't seem to be raining yet!" said Jim. "No," laughed Rosie. "The big cloud has gone and it's sunny again!" "The sun can dry Tootle's clothes now!" said Jim.

7. "We'll hang the clothes up for Tootle!" said Jim. "He will be pleased," said Rosie. "I'll put the clothes on the line and you put the pegs on, Rosie," said Jim.

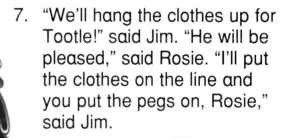

8. "Quack!" shouted Duck. "Oh no!" said Rosie. "Here comes an even bigger cloud!" "I felt some rain!" said Jim. "It must have fallen off the cloud."

9. "Quick!" said Jim. "We'd better get under our cloth again!" "Oh dear," said Rosie. "Look at Tootle's clothes! They are getting very wet!"

10. "The big cloud has gone," said Jim. "And the rain has stopped," said Rosie. "What a naughty cloud for wetting Tootle's clothes!" said Jim.

11. "Quack!" said Duck. "Duck says Tootle's coming!" said Jim. "We must hide!" said Rosie. "Gosh!" said Neil. "How did my clothes get back on the line?"

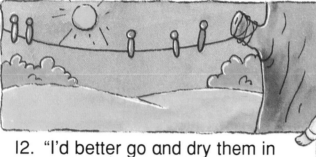

12. "I'd better go and dry them in the laundrette," said Neil. "We'll go too!" said Jim. "It's very sunny again!" said Rosie. "I'll take my sunglasses."

13. "There are some little white clouds," said Jim. "Do you think they will drop rain on us?" "No!" said Rosie. "Those clouds are too small to drop rain." "They are very pretty clouds!" said Jim.

14. "There's a funny cloud!" said Jim. "That cloud looks like you, Jim!" giggled Rosie. "I hope you won't rain on us, Jim cloud!"

15. "It's raining again!" giggled Rosie. "We can keep dry under this bush." "Look at all the people keeping out of the rain!" said Rosie. "Nobody wants to get wet!"

16. "They are very naughty clouds for trying to make everybody wet!" said Jim. "There's Tootle putting his clothes in a drying machine," said Rosie.

17. "There's a big, funny cloud," said Jim. "That's not a cloud!" giggled Rosie. "That's smoke coming from a chimney!" "At least the smoke cloud isn't dripping rain on us!" said Jim.

18. "Tootle's coming out!" said Rosie. "Quick!" said Jim. "Where can we hide?" Can YOU see Rosie and Jim?

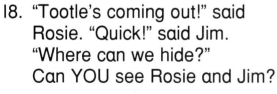

19. "My flowers could do with a bit of extra water," said the flower lady. "I'm glad somebody likes the rain!" laughed Neil. "Maybe the clouds aren't so naughty after all!" said Jim.

20. "There!" said Neil. "At last I've got some lovely clean clothes!" "Look at our cloth," said Rosie. "The rain has made a big puddle on it," said Jim.

21. "We don't want this puddle!" said Jim. "Let's throw it away!" said Rosie. "Ready Jim? One, two, three … " WHOOSH!

22. "Oh no!" said Neil. "I don't believe it! I'll have to start all over again!"
"Oh dear, Jim!"
"Oh dear, Rosie!"

Storm in a Bottle

Here's an activity for in the bath or out in the garden!

You will need:
some paper
pens and pencils
safety scissors
an empty plastic bottle
paste or sticky tape

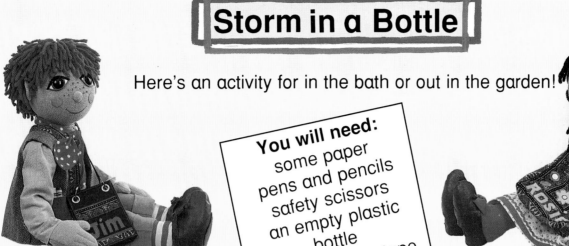

1. Draw a raincloud shape on a piece of paper.

2. Ask an adult to carefully cut the shape out.

3. Paste your cloud onto an empty plastic bottle.

4. Fill the bottle with water.

5. Now, when you turn the bottle upside down – it pours with rain!

Ride in the Sky

One day, just as Rosie and Jim were walking up a hill, a bird flew round and round their heads.

"Quack!" said Duck.

"Look," said Jim. "Look at that bird flying high in the sky."

"Quack!" said Duck.

"Ah, poor Duck, I think he wishes he could fly as well," said Rosie.

Just then a cloud came past.

"I can fly round hills," said the cloud. "Would you like a ride?"

"Quack!" said Duck.

"Yes please!" said Rosie and Jim.

Rosie and Jim and Duck got on the cloud.

"You're all soft!" giggled Jim. "And fluffy!"

"Off we go," said the cloud.

The cloud flew away from the hill, and Rosie and Jim looked down.

"There's a brown field!" said Jim. "With brown flowers."

"Oh dear," said Rosie. "I think those flowers need some water."

"I'll give them some of my rain!" said the cloud.

The cloud rained on the flowers.

"Thank you, cloud!" shouted the flowers.

"Look over there, Rosie!" said Jim. "I can see the sea!"

"And there are some big sea clouds," said the cloud.

"Hello, sea clouds!" shouted Rosie and Jim as they waved.

Soon they were back on the hill.
"We had a lovely ride!" said Rosie.
"Thank you very much!" said Jim.
"Bye bye," said the cloud.
"Quack!" said Duck.

13

The Wettest Cloud!

1. One sunny day Rosie and Jim and Duck were out walking when Duck shouted "QUACK!" "Oh no!" said Jim. "There's a dark cloud coming! It might rain on us!"

2. "It's only a little cloud," said Rosie. "It won't be able to rain very much!" "Here it comes!" said Jim. "And I think it's raining a lot!"

3. "Quick, run!" said Jim. "We can hide under this tree," said Rosie. "Please wait for me!" said the cloud.

4. "Don't come near us!" said Jim. "We don't want to be wet!" "Everybody runs away from me!" said the cloud. "I only want to be friendly!"

14

5. "Quack!" said Duck. "Duck isn't running away!" giggled Jim. "Our Duck likes getting wet!" laughed Rosie. "What a nice duck," said the cloud.

6. "Maybe we can find some more people who need a cloud!" said Jim. "Come with us, cloud!" said Rosie. "But don't rain on us!"

7. "There's a muddy old tractor!" said Jim. "He's very muddy!" "I've been ploughing a muddy field today," said the tractor. "I wish I could be clean again."

8. "Maybe our friend could help!" said Rosie. "Of course I can," said the cloud. "I can give you a wash!"

15

9. "That's better!" said the tractor. "Thank you very much!" "It was fun!" said the cloud. "Let's find somebody else to help now," said Jim.

10. "Quack!" said Duck. "These flowers look a bit floppy," said Rosie. "We need a nice drink of water," said the flowers. "Here I come!" said the cloud.

11. "Hooray!" said the flowers. "That's just what we needed!" "I like helping people," said the cloud. "Who's next?"

12. "Quack quack!" said Duck. "There are some of Duck's friends!" said Jim. "Quack!" said the ducks. "Their pond has dried up," said Rosie. "Can you help, cloud?"

16

13. "This is going to take a lot of water!" said Jim. "I'll do my best!" said the cloud. "Get ready, ducks!"

14. "There you are, ducks!" said Rosie. "Your pond is full again!" "Quack!" said the ducks. "Gosh!" said the cloud. "I don't think I can rain anymore. I've run out of water!"

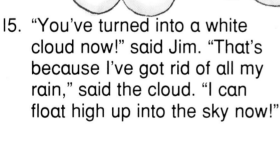

15. "You've turned into a white cloud now!" said Jim. "That's because I've got rid of all my rain," said the cloud. "I can float high up into the sky now!"

16. "Up she goes!" said Rosie. "Thank you for helping everybody!" said Jim. "Thank you for helping me!" said the cloud.

Different Clouds

ALL CLOUD PHOTOGRAPHS © S.D. BURT

The New Room

1. "Look at Tootle!" giggled Rosie. "He's putting on some funny old clothes!" "I like his old shoes!" said Jim.

2. "What is he going to do today?" asked Rosie. "Whatever it is, it looks like fun." said Jim. "Come on, Rosie, we'll go too!" "Bye bye, Duck!" "Quack!" said Duck.

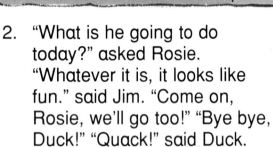

3. "Thanks for coming, Neil," said the lady. "We've got a lot to do!" "It'll be a nice surprise for Fred when he comes home!" laughed Neil.

4. "Tootle is making a surprise for somebody!" whispered Rosie. "Somebody called Fred!" said Jim. "I wonder what the surprise is?"

20

5. "We'd better move all the furniture first," said the lady. "I'll help with the sofa," said Neil. "We'd better keep out of the way!" said Rosie.

6. "Oh dear!" said Neil. "I think I'm a bit stuck!" "You'll have to climb in the window!" laughed the lady. "What is funny old Tootle doing?" giggled Jim.

7. "We can sneak past the sofa!" said Jim. "Ragdolls are smaller than Tootles!" said Rosie. "Look! There's Tootle coming in!"

8. "Painting is the first job!" said the lady. "Here's a brush." "Let's do the ceiling first!" said Neil. "We can stand on this box."

9. "Oh dear!" said the lady. "I'm afraid the paint is dripping down a lot!" "Never mind," said Neil. "These are my oldest clothes." "Tootle is getting all messy!" giggled Rosie. "What a good game!" laughed Jim.

10. "We've just got the wood round the floor to paint now," said Neil. "How would you like a cup of tea first?" asked the lady. "Yes please," said Neil. "Come on then!" said the lady.

11. "Maybe we could paint the wood by the floor!" said Jim. "We must be careful not to get messy like Tootle!" said Rosie.

12. Backwards, forwards, up and down, We carefully brush the paint around. Go along the edges, corners too, Paint makes everything look brand new!

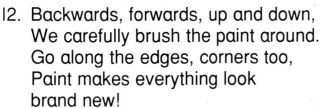

13. "Shh, Jim!" said Rosie. "They're coming back!" "We must find a place to hide!" said Jim. CAN YOU SEE ROSIE AND JIM?

14. "Gosh!" said the lady. "The painting seems to have finished by itself." "I wonder how that could have happened?" asked Neil. "We know!" whispered Rosie. "It was us!" giggled Jim.

15. "The wallpaper is the next job," said the woman. "I've got the big pot of sticky paste ready," said Neil. "Sticky paste!" said Jim. "For making things sticky!" giggled Rosie.

16. "I'll put the paste on!" said Neil. "Oh no! The paper has rolled up!" "Tootle has got the sticky paste on his shirt!" laughed Jim.

17. "Pass the paper to me and I'll stick it up," said the lady. "The paper is very pretty," said Rosie. "Lots of flowers!" said Jim.

18. "Ooh, this game is sticky-sticky lovely," said Rosie. "The room looks all lovely now. Oh, but look at Tootle! He doesn't look lovely, does he?" "No. Oh dear!" said Jim.

19. "Hold the ladder steady while I do the top bit," said the lady. "I've got it!" said Neil. "Jim!" giggled Rosie. "Be careful!"

20. "There!" said the lady. "What a smart job we've made!" "I hope Fred likes it," said Neil. "Let's get the furniture back in!"

21. "What's happened to your back?" laughed the lady. "Oh my goodness!" said Neil. "How did I do that?"

22. "Right, that's everything back in place!" said Neil. "Just in time!" said the lady. "I can see Fred coming."

23. "Hello!" said the man. "What a lovely surprise! Our room looks brand new!" "Neil helped me!" said the lady. "And we helped too!" said Rosie and Jim.

24. "You must stay for a big tea!"
said Fred. "Thank you," said Neil.
"We'd better get back to the
Ragdoll and see Duck!" said Jim.
"Come on!" said Rosie.

25. "Here, Duck," said Rosie.
"We made you a present from
the wallpaper!" "Quack!" said
Duck. "Here comes Tootle!"
said Jim. "He must have
finished his tea."

26. "Tootle has gone to sleep!"
said Rosie. "He is tired
from all his painting!" "Look
at his funny old shoes!" said
Jim. "Did you like painting,
shoes?" "I think they did!"
laughed Rosie.

Decorate a Room

Can YOU make a lovely sticky mess as well?

The Paper Caper

One day Rosie and Jim and Duck were in an old house.

"Look!" said Rosie. "There's some wallpaper and paste. Maybe we could decorate the house and make it nice!"

"Let's have a go!" said Jim. "Come on, Duck."

"Quack!" said Duck.

Jim unrolled the roll of paper and Rosie put some sticky paste onto it.

"There you are Jim, see if that will stick to the wall," said Rosie.

"Yes!" said Jim. "It looks very nice! Let's do another bit."

Rosie pasted more bits of paper and Jim put them on the walls.

Soon they had finished. They had a rest and looked round the room.

"It looks very smart, Jim," said Rosie.

"We did a good job, didn't we?" said Jim.

"Jim," said Rosie. "Where's Duck?"

"Duck!" shouted Rosie and Jim. "Duck, where are you?"

"There's a funny lump in the wall," said Rosie.

"Quack!" said the lump.

"The lump went quack!" said Jim. "I heard it!"

Rosie and Jim pulled the paper off the lump.

"It's Duck!" said Rosie.

"I must have covered you in paper!" said Jim. "I'm sorry, Duck!"

"It's time to go home now," said Rosie. "Oh no! Somebody's taken the door away."

"Gosh!" said Jim. "I'm sure there was a door when we came in!"

"Quack!" said Duck.

"What has Duck found?" asked Rosie.

"There is a lump on the wall under the wallpaper," said Jim. "I'll give it a pull!"

"I'll help you, Jim," said Rosie. "One, two, three … pull!"

There was a big ripping sound!

"Hooray! We've found the door!" said Jim.

"Come on everybody!" laughed Rosie. "It's time to go home!"

29

The Flower House

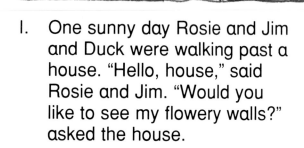

1. One sunny day Rosie and Jim and Duck were walking past a house. "Hello, house," said Rosie and Jim. "Would you like to see my flowery walls?" asked the house.

2. "I can't see any flowers," said Jim. "That's the trouble," said the house. "They're inside. Look!" "They are very pretty!" said Rosie.

3. "I wish I had flowery walls outside!" said the house. "There are lots of flowers in the garden," said Jim. "It's not the same as flowery walls," said the house.

4. "Quack!" said Duck. "What are you doing in my shed?" asked the house. "Duck has found some glue," said Rosie. "And a brush."

5. "We can stick some flowers on your walls!" said Jim. "On the outside?" asked the house. "Why not?" said Rosie. "Why not indeed," laughed the house.

6. "We'll put some paste on first," said Rosie. "Tee hee!" giggled the house. "That tickles!" "Make sure you put plenty on, Rosie!" said Jim.

7. "Now I'll stick the flowers on!" said Jim. "Oh dear, I can't reach very high!" "You'd better stand on me!" said Rosie. "Don't fall on the sticky walls, Jim!"

8. "Oh no!" said Rosie. "You're too heavy, Jim! You've been eating too many sausages." "Help!" said Jim. "I'm wobbling!"

9. SPLAT! "Why haven't I fallen down?" asked Jim. "You've stuck to my sticky wall!" said the house. "You are funny, Jim!" giggled Rosie.

10. "Come on, Duck," said Rosie. "We'll pull Jim down. One, two, three … pull!"

11. "I'm all sticky now," said Jim. "Hang on," said Rosie. "I've got an idea!"

12. "There!" said Rosie. "You have flowery walls inside AND outside!"

13. "Thank you. I'm now the floweriest house that ever was!"

14. "And we are the floweriest Duck and Jim there ever was," laughed Jim. "Quack!" said Duck.

33

Friends

1. "Quack!" said Duck. "Wake up, Rosie!" said Jim. "It's morning time!" "Good morning, Jim," said Rosie. "It's very dark in here!" said Neil. "I'll open the curtains."

2. "Gosh, who's that moving behind me?" said Neil. "Silly me, it's only my shadow!"

3. "Look!" said Jim. "There are two people behind us!" "They must be our shadows," said Rosie. "They are like magic people!" giggled Jim.

4. "Hello, magic people!" said Rosie. "They are waving back at us!" said Jim. "That one is copying you, Jim!" "And that one is copying you, Rosie!" giggled Jim.

34

5. "I'll get some milk for my breakfast," said Neil. "Let's go with Tootle!" said Jim. "Look!" said Rosie. "Tootle has his magic person with him!"

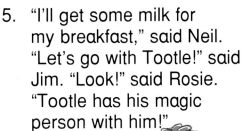

6. "My magic Jim is coming with me!" said Jim. "And my magic Rosie is coming with me!" said Rosie. "Our magic friends are very quiet, Jim!"

7. "These flowers have got some magic friends too!" said Jim. "So has the tree!" said Rosie.

8. "Let's have a race with our magic friends," said Jim. "Ready … GO!" shouted Rosie. "Gosh!" said Jim. "Our magic friends can run as fast as we can!"

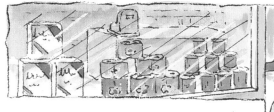

9. "There's Tootle going into a shop," said Rosie. "Come on magic friends, we'll go in too!" said Jim.

10. "Lovely day, isn't it?" said the shop lady. "Beautiful," said Neil. "Where has Tootle's shadow friend gone?" asked Jim. "Ours have gone too!" said Rosie.

11. "Magic friends? Where are you?" asked Rosie and Jim. "They are not behind these big boxes," said Rosie. "And not hiding in the apples," said Jim.

12 "I give up!" said Jim. "I can't see them at all." "Thank you for the milk," said Neil. "Goodbye," said the shop lady. "Tootle's going," said Rosie.

13. "Look!" said Jim. "Tootle's shadow has come back!" "He must have been waiting for Tootle outside the shop!" giggled Rosie.

14. "Here are our shadow friends too!" said Jim. "Thank you for waiting for us," said Rosie. "Look, Jim, they are holding hands just like us!"

15. "There's a big cloud in the sky," said Jim. "The sun has gone!" "Our shadow friends have gone too," said Rosie. "How strange!"

16. "Now the sun is back!" said Rosie. "And so are the shadow friends," said Jim.

17. "Rosie, look at our shadow friends now," said Jim. "They are very long!" giggled Rosie. "Look at those long legs!" laughed Jim.

18. "Look at Tootle's shirt!" said Rosie. "It's got a magic friend too!"

19. "I've made a funny face for the shirt!" said Rosie. "Let's hold it up!" said Jim.

20. "There's somebody on the boat!" said Neil. "I wonder who it could be?" "Tootle's coming!" giggled Jim. "Shhh, Rosie!"

21. "There's nobody there!" said Neil. "It was just my shirt making a funny shadow!"

22 "Look, Duck," said Rosie. "We've got some magic friends called shadows." "You have a magic shadow friend too, Duck!" said Jim. "What would your friend say if he could talk?" "Quack!" said Duck.

Whose Shadow?

Some shadows have come loose! Can you see which shadow belongs to which person or thing? Draw a line to link up the objects with their shadows.

Rosie's Funny Game

One day, Jim was doing a drawing when he saw a strange shadow on the table.

"There's something wobbling over my picture!" said Jim. "There must be something funny going past the window."

Jim looked out of the window, but there was nothing there.

"I must have dreamed it!" Jim said, and he did some more drawing.

Just then there was another funny shadow!

"Another shadow!" said Jim. "I'll look out of the window again!"

Jim looked out of the window again, but there was still nobody there.

Jim did some more drawing, and there was another shadow!

"Look at this shadow!" said Jim.

"I know what that shadow is! It's Duck!"

Jim looked out of the window.

"Duck! Duck!" he shouted. Then he heard some giggling.

Jim looked down and saw Rosie hiding with Duck.

"Rosie!" said Jim. "Were you making some funny wobbly shadows?"

"Tee hee!" giggled Rosie. "I was playing a game!"

"And I saw Duck's shadow too!" said Jim. "Were you playing too, Duck?"

"Quack!" said Duck.

"What a funny game!" laughed Jim.

Shadow Shadow!

Horsey horsey, don't you stop,
Just let your feet go clippity clop.
Your tail goes swish and the
wheels go round,
Giddy up, we're homeward bound.

Shadow shadow, come with me
Follow me around the tree.
Faster and faster, round and round,
Follow me without a sound.

42

Shadow Fun

I've made a caterpillar, Rosie!

I've made a dancing lady, Jim!

You can have fun making shadows.

Cut out some funny people and animals from card and then make their shadows dance on the wall!

You can even use your hands to make shadows!

43

Silly Shadows

1. "What a nice sunny day," said Jim. "We've got good shadows today," said Rosie. "There's mine." "And there's mine," said Jim. "Quack!" said Duck.

2. "Gosh!" said Jim. "My shadow has run away!" "There goes my shadow too!" said Rosie. "I wonder why they've gone?"

3. "We'll have to catch them!" said Jim. "Come on, Duck," said Rosie.

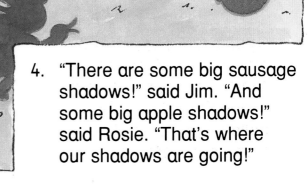

4. "There are some big sausage shadows!" said Jim. "And some big apple shadows!" said Rosie. "That's where our shadows are going!"

5. "My shadow wants to eat a sausage!" said Jim. "And my shadow is trying to catch an apple!" said Rosie.

6. "Quack!" said Duck. "Look!" said Jim. "There are some balloons!" "Hello!" said the balloons. "Your shadows have been chasing our shadows!"

7. "Silly shadows!" laughed Jim. "You thought you were chasing sausages and apples!"

8 "You'd better stay with me, Rosie shadow," said Rosie. "And Jim shadow should stay with me!" laughed Jim. "And our shadows had better stay with us!" said the balloons. "We don't want them to get eaten!"

Neil's Big Band

1. "Quack!" said Duck.
"We're stopping, Rosie!" said Jim. "Where are we?" asked Rosie. "Let's see!" said Jim.

2. "It's market day!" said Neil. "I wonder if anybody wants me to play some tunes?" "Tootle is going to play tunes," said Jim. "On his tootler!" giggled Rosie.

3. "Hello, Neil!" said the café man. "I haven't seen you for ages!" "Hello, George," said Neil. "Are you busy?" "It's a bit quiet today," said the café man.

4. "How about a tune to liven things up?" asked the café man. "All right!" said Neil. "Tootle is getting his tootler out!" said Jim. "He's going to tootle!" giggled Rosie.

46

5. "I want to hear the music!" said a boy. "I'll have a cup of tea while I'm here," said the lady. "Certainly, madam," said the café man.

6. "Look!" said Jim. "Tootle's little tune pipe has fallen from his pocket." "Let's borrow it!" said Rosie.

7. "I'd like to buy this guitar, please," said a lady. "And I'd like that tambourine!" said the girl. "Here you are," said the man.

8. "Let's play some music now," said the girl. "I wish we had somebody to play with," said the lady. "We can find them somebody to play with!" giggled Rosie.

9. PEEP PEEP! went Jim on the whistle. "I can hear some music!" said the girl. "Where?" asked the lady. "It was over here," said the girl.

47

10. "They are following us!" whispered Rosie. PEEP! went Jim again. "Come on Mum," said the girl. "I heard the music again!"

11. "There!" said the girl. "There's the music!" "They've found Tootle!" giggled Jim.

12. "We heard you blowing your whistle," said the lady. "I didn't blow a whistle!" laughed Neil. "Do you want to play along with me?" "Yes, please!" said the girl.

13. "We found somebody for Tootle to play with!" said Jim. "Let's find some more!" giggled Rosie.

14. "Look in that car!" said Jim. "Some boys with music boxes!" said Rosie. "I want them to hear Tootle!"

15. TWEEET!

16. "What was that noise?" asked the boys. "Wind down the window and look!"

17. "Dad! There's some music playing!" said the boys. "Can we join in?" "Why don't you go and ask?" laughed their father. "Here they come!" giggled Jim.

49

18. "Can we play our violins with you?" asked the boys. "Of course!" said Neil. "The more the merrier!" "There are lots of people watching now!" said Jim.

19. "Who else can we find to play?" asked Rosie. "There are some more people playing," said Jim. "And they have a nice dog!"

20. "Hello, dog!" said Jim. "Can you hear Tootle playing his music?" asked Rosie. "Woof!" said the dog.

21. "What is Merlin barking at?" asked the girl. "I think he's heard something!" said the man. "Listen!" said the girl. "I can hear it too!"

22. "Your music sounds good!" said the girl. "Can we play too?" "This band is getting bigger and bigger!" laughed Neil.

23. "Two teas, a cake and a sandwich, please!" said a man. "Can I have a fizzy drink and a cake?" asked a girl. "And some crisps too!" "I'm going as fast as I can!" laughed the café man.

24. "The café man is getting very busy now!" giggled Rosie. "Look!" said Jim. "He's dropped a sausage!" "Here, Merlin!" giggled Rosie. "Do you want it?"

25. "That was fun!" said Neil. "Thanks for joining in, everybody!" "Goodbye!" they all said. "Tootle liked having all his music friends playing," giggled Rosie.

26. "Phew!" said the café man. "I've never been so busy!" "I'm glad the music helped," said Neil.

27. "Don't go yet!" chuckled the café man. "I've got a surprise for you!" "Ooh, a surprise, Rosie!" said Jim. "What is it?" asked Rosie.

28. "What a brilliant tea!" said Neil. "Cheers!" said the café man. "Yummy sausages, Rosie!" said Jim. "And slurpy orange juice, Jim," giggled Rosie.

52

The Rosie and Jim Band

You can be in the Rosie and Jim band as well! Play your instruments and march around.

Ask an adult to put some music on for you.

Pretend you are playing the music you hear!
Can you play softly? Can you play loudly? Fast and slow?
Try to stop when the music stops, and then start again when the music starts.

53

Follow the Drum

One day Rosie and Jim and Duck found some noisy instruments in a field.

"Hello!" said Rosie. "What are you doing?"

"We are trying to play a tune," said the trumpet. "It goes like this!"
PARP PARPY PARP!

"No, no!" said the flute. "That's too slow! It should be faster, like this."
TOOTLY TOOTLY TOOT!

"You're both too fast!" said the tuba. "It should be like this."
OOM-PAH OOM-PAH!

"What happens if you all play together?" asked Jim.

"We'll show you," said the trumpet. "Ready, everybody? Off we go!"
PARP TOOTLE OOM-PAH!

"What a noise!" giggled Rosie. "It doesn't sound much like music!"

Just then Duck found something in the bushes.

"Quack!" said Duck.

"There's a big old drum!" said Jim. "Can you play a tune?"

"Not me," said the drum. "I just go BOOM BOOM BOOM."

"But that's exactly what you all need!" said Jim.

"What?" said everybody.

"Let Duck bang the drum," said Jim.

Duck banged the big drum. BOOM BOOM BOOM.

"Now everybody join in with the drum," said Jim.

"Not too fast and not too slow!" said Rosie.

"All right," said the tuba and they all started playing. OOM PARP TOOTLE OOM PARP TOOTLE

"That sounds better!" said Jim. "Now you are all playing at the right speed."

"Good old drum!" they all cheered.

55

The Poorly Piano

1. One sunny day Rosie, Jim and Duck found an old piano. "Hello!" said Rosie. "Can you play us a tune?"

2. "I'll try," said the piano. "But you have to press my keys first." "Keys?" asked Jim. "Those long black and white sticks at the front," said the piano.

3. "Ready, Rosie?" asked Jim. "Off we go!"
PLINK PLINK CROAK!

56

4. "You made a croak noise!" said Rosie. "I'm not very well," said the piano. "There's something wrong with my insides." "We'll have a look," said Jim.

5. "Gosh!" said Jim. "What a lot of strings and bits." "Look!" said Rosie. "I can see some eyes!" CROAK! came a noise.

6. "It's a little frog!" said Jim. "Come here, I'll get you out." "So that's what the matter was!" said the piano. "He must have been stuck inside."

7. "Let's try and play another tune!" said Rosie. "Off we go again!" PLINK PLINK TWEET!

8. "There's somebody else in there!" said Jim. "It's a little bird!" said Rosie. "Come on out, little bird!"

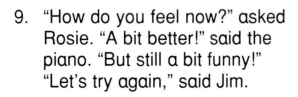

9. "How do you feel now?" asked Rosie. "A bit better!" said the piano. "But still a bit funny!" "Let's try again," said Jim.

10. PLINK PLINK SQUEAK! "There's still somebody in there!" said Rosie. "A mouse!" said Jim. "Squeak!" said the mouse.

11. "Try me again!" said the piano.
"I feel much better!"
PLINKY PLINKY PLONK
PLONK!
"You sound much better too!"
said Jim.

12. "Who would like to sing
a song?" asked the piano.
"Croak!" went the frog.
"Tweet!" went the bird.
"Squeak!" went the mouse.
"Yes, please!" said Rosie and
Jim. "Quack!" said Duck.

13. "Let's sing our favourite song then!"
said the piano. "One … two … three …"

Rosie and Jim, Rosie and Jim,
Looking for music everyday.
Rosie and Jim, Rosie and Jim,
And we're all singing along.

Who Plays What?

Rosie and Jim have gone to see a band play – but the instruments have all been moved!

Can you see who should be playing which instrument?

Peep-Bo Back

Can you play peep-bo back through the book to find these things on the pages?